The Avro Vulcan

Britain's Cold War Warrior

The Avro Vulcan

Britain's Cold War Warrior

MIDLAND

An imprint of
Ian Allan Publishing

Foreword by Air Chief Marshal Sir Michael Knight KCB AFC FRAeS
Chairman, Vulcan to the Sky Trust

Philip Birtles

Author's Note

When a schoolboy, my ambition was to join the Royal Air Force and fly the Vulcan. I had first seen this beautiful and powerful aircraft at the Farnborough Air Show in 1953 and had been impressed from then on. As I matured, my preference was for a more stable family life, rather than being posted around various RAF bases in what I perceived to be an unsettling existence. I therefore decided to enter the aerospace industry, starting as a student of the de Havilland Aeronautical School, gaining an excellent engineering training, and had no regrets about not flying with the RAF.

In later years I did regain my ambition of learning to fly, even if it was only to PPL standard, but I continued to have an interest in the Vulcan, which is probably only second in public popularity to Concorde. It is therefore with great interest and hope that by the time this book is published, Vulcan XH558 will be in the air.

For assistance with this book I would like to thank my long-term friend and past colleague at BAe Woodford, Harry Holmes; Andrew Renwick and the archive team at the RAF Museum; Mrs Sharon Cowley at the Air Historical Branch, Bentley Priory; Rusty Drewett, Denis Parker and Alan Rolfe of VTS at Bruntingthorpe; Dave Griffiths and Richard Clarkson of the Vulcan Restoration Trust at Southend. It is good to be working again with Nick Grant and Peter Waller of Ian Allan Publishing, even though they gave me a near-impossible deadline to achieve.

My wife Martha has been very supportive during the preparation of this book, and I therefore thank her for all her help, particularly with her computer skills.

Philip Birtles
April, 2007

First published 2007

ISBN (10) 1 85780 269 1

ISBN (13) 978 1 85780 269 6

Published by Midland Publishing

An imprint of Ian Allan Publishing Ltd, Riverdene Business Park, Molesey Road, Hersham, Surrey KT12 4RG

Printed by Ian Allan Printing Ltd, Riverdene Business Park, Molesey Road, Hersham, Surrey KT12 4RG

Code: 0707/B2

Visit the Ian Allan Publishing website at www.ianallanpublishing.co.uk

Contents

Foreword
Air Chief Marshal Sir Michael Knight KCB AFC FRAeS

If there is any justice in the world, by the time this book is published, Vulcan XH558 will again be airborne and entering a 10 to 15 year period on the UK air display circuit. That this has been possible is due to the very professional efforts of a small number of people, who have given up to seven years of their lives to deliver one of the most complex projects of aircraft restoration ever undertaken. Indeed, it is doubtful whether such an ambitious programme has ever been completed anywhere in the world, and throughout the course of the project there were many who deemed it an impossible achievement.

It goes without saying that the task presented the Vulcan to the Sky (VTS) team with a constant series of challenges, which might well have deterred all but the most dedicated of aviation enthusiasts. Those challenges covered the range of possible problem areas – from research to programme planning, organisation to management, the recruitment of skilled staff, logistics and engineering. And underpinning all this was a remarkable funding effort which, over the years, resulted in the raising of around £6 million. Key to this was a grant of £2,734,000 from the Heritage Lottery Fund, which kept the project alive at a particularly critical stage;

and the involvement and continuing support of the fund was a source of continued encouragement to VTS. That said, the balance of the project's funding had to come from the general public in a fundraising effort that is thought to have been one of the most impressive ever for a non-humanitarian charity in this country. Some 20,000 extremely loyal 'Friends' and members of the VTST Club were joined by individual donors, with contributions ranging from a project-saving grant of half a million pounds by the philanthropist, Sir Jack Hayward, to a 92p contribution by a young schoolboy at the end of the ceremony marking the aircraft's first appearance in the open air for some 13 years.

That event marked a dramatic change of fortune for the project. From a continuing battle to raise funds to meet increasing costs, to near financial meltdown, it was saved at the very last minute, by an unprecedented influx of money. With renewed interest by the media, a possible wake on 31 August 2006 was transformed into a day of genuine rejoicing as, with great ceremony and before a large crowd of well-wishers, XH558 was rolled out of her hangar and rolled back again so that work could continue uninterrupted. The dramatic appearance overhead of the Lancaster from the Battle of Britain Memorial Flight was particularly felicitous, being one of Avro Chief Designer Roy Chadwick's most famous creations that he worked on prior to his untimely death in August 1947.

2007 will be another memorable year for the project, and given the sort of good fortune it surely deserves, will see Vulcan XH558 safely restored to her natural environment in her new guise as G-VLCN on the Civil Aircraft Register. She will then, once again, be free to thrill the millions who will see her each year at air displays around the country or in transit to and from them. These most popular of events will undoubtedly benefit, as the instantly recognisable sound of the Spitfire and Hurricane and the impressive dignity of the Lancaster are complemented by the awesome sight of a Vulcan, paying its own moving tribute to the valour and foresight of planners, the talents of aircraft designers and engineers and the steadfast determination of a generation of airmen whose proud task it was to help prevent conflict.

To sustain that effort, there will be a continuing need for fundraising if the aircraft is to realise her full potential as an icon of British design and engineering.

It is also a living tribute to those many in the aerospace industry and the Royal Air Force who ensured that the Vulcan played a full part throughout the so-called 'Cold War' in the ultimately successful Alliance strategy of deterrence. At the very end of their in-service life, Vulcans and their gallant air and ground crews also contributed to the success of the South Atlantic conflict of 1982 by undertaking dramatic bombing raids on the airfield, radars and missile sites at Port Stanley.

It has always been VTS's objective that the aircraft will, for many years, inspire the country's young people to appreciate the history of the second half of the century past, and perhaps, as aircrew and engineers or in any other capacity, to consider careers in aerospace. To keep the Vulcan thus in the public eye, it is hoped that the aircraft's unique potential for sponsorship will attract one or more to support it throughout its second 'life' in the air.

As we say in the aviation business: 'Onwards and Upwards'!

The end of World War 2 gave hope to the nations involved that production of the war machine would cease and their economies could rebuild, leading to peaceful, global coexistence.

This was not to be.

Whereas matters surrounding Japan's defeat were relatively easy to settle in terms of the country's disarmament and temporary occupation by the USA, the situation in Europe was far more complicated. Nazi Germany had been defeated on all fronts, and while the Western Allies' intentions were to occupy enemy territory on a temporary basis, Stalin's armed forces swept onwards. Instead of liberating Eastern Europe, the Red Army occupied countries such as Poland and Czechoslovakia by force, the Fascist occupiers of those nations replaced by an equally harsh regime of Soviet communism. After the fall of the Third Reich, the Soviet Union's military strength continued to grow and her first atomic test in 1949 saw her become a superpower in a period the world would soon come to know as 'The Cold War'.

At the end of the war, the Allies had divided Berlin into separate zones: Britain, France and the USA were responsible for western parts of the city whereas the Russians were responsible for the east. To protect their interests, the Russians built the infamous Berlin Wall which divided the city – the capital being divided by the major powers – and Eastern Europe was defined as being behind the 'Iron Curtain' where new puppet communist regimes provided military and political support to the Soviet Union. The Berlin Blockade in 1948 made it necessary for the Allies to implement Operation Plainfare, an airlift in which the capital was supplied with supplies by air through defined corridors. The operation provided tons of much needed fuel and provisions into the beleaguered city before the Russians reopened access.

The Allies came to the decision that there was an urgent need for a rearmament programme to counter the threat from the USSR, a threat which included nuclear air strikes and massive armoured forces capable of rapid and devastating attacks. While fighters were needed to intercept high-flying Soviet bombers, the Allies required a nuclear counter threat as a suitable deterrent to Russia. America had already developed the first atomic bomb which was used against Japan, and perfected the hydrogen bomb – which Britain had helped develop the technology for – but the only method of delivery at the time was by air.

The English Electric Canberra, Britain's first jet bomber, first flew on 13 May 1949 and, with initial delivery to RAF Binbrook in Lincolnshire on 25 May 1951, entered service with 101 Squadron. The Canberra was viewed as a replacement for the highly successful wartime de Havilland Mosquito bomber in the unarmed high speed and high altitude role, but was limited to tactical operations due to its modest load carrying capability and range. To counter the Soviet threat, Britain required a long range, high altitude strategic bomber capable of carrying nuclear weapons to major military and infrastructure targets within the USSR in co-operation with the USA and France.

The government issued Specification B.35/46, which outlined the overall requirement. This was considered to be fairly high risk due to the lack of knowledge at the time, particularly with the performance of swept wing aircraft and near sonic speeds at high altitudes. At the time, the RAF were operating Avro Lincoln bombers, a development of the wartime Avro Lancaster, and lend-lease Boeing Washingtons from the USA which evolved from the B-29, but both were slow propeller-driven aircraft using World War 2 technology whose

Two prototypes of the Short Sperrin were built, with the first, VX158, making its maiden flight from Aldergrove on 10 August 1951. With the Valiant being preferred as the interim jet bomber, VX158 was allocated to engine development with the de Havilland Engine Company. A Gyron engine replaced the Avon in the port lower nacelle in 1955, followed by a second Gyron engine in the lower starboard nacelle. The aircraft was scrapped at Hatfield in 1958 following cancellation of the Gyron engine programme.
(*de Havilland photo*)

capabilities were seen as inadequate in comparison to operational Russian strategic bombers.

In the event that there would be problems achieving the full specification, an interim low risk Spec B.14/46 was issued. Shorts Aircraft responded with the SA.4 Sperrin and was judged to be the best of the proposals, a contract being awarded for two prototypes. This interim specification called for a range of 3,350 nautical miles with a bomb load of 10,000lb, and effective at an altitude of 45,000 feet. The aircraft was designed around the bomb bay of 30ft in length, 10 feet in width and 10 feet in depth to accommodate the weapons of the time. The crew of five were housed in a pressurised cabin and bomb aiming was conducted with the advanced HS2 radar with a visual bombing station in the nose as a standby. Design and construction was conventional with the capability for rapid quantity production and easy maintenance. The major recognisable feature was the vertical pairing of the Rolls-Royce Avon engines in wing-mounted pods, and this proved to be a useful layout for many of the aircraft's later duties. The all-metal airframe had straight wings with modest sweepback on the leading edge and a conventional tail layout.

Construction of two prototypes and a structural test specimen began in Belfast in 1948, but completion of the first prototype VX158 was delayed due to the transfer of the design department from Rochester to Belfast and was not completed until the late spring of 1951. Before the maiden flight on 10 August 1951, a protracted programme of engine runs and taxiing was required, with a move by road from Sydenham to Aldergrove for flight trials. The aircraft performed well and could have entered service with the RAF as a Lincoln replacement but George Edwards of Vickers at Weybridge offered the Type 660, better known as the Valiant. An alternative interim bomber, the Valiant was accepted by the government in February 1949 with Specification B.9/48 written specifically to accommodate it.

The Valiant could be operational before the Sperrin whose prototypes were plagued by delays and were less aerodynamically advanced than the requirements set-out in Specification B.35/46. With the recent investment in an advanced high-speed wind tunnel and slab milling machines, Vickers was able to quickly start design and production of the four Rolls-Royce Avon powered Valiants with the first flight from Wisley on 18 May 1951. This signalled the end of the Sperrin programme which found little application apart from the first prototype which was used as an engine testbed by the de Havilland Engine Company at Hatfield for the Gyron axial flow jet engine. Trials commenced on 7 July 1955 supported by second prototype VX161 as a spares source, the Sperrin to be eventually scrapped at Hatfield in 1958 after the Gyron programme was cancelled as an economy measure.

A total of three prototypes and 108 production Valiants were built with the first delivery to 232 Operational Conversion Unit (OCU) at Gaydon in early 1955 followed by a second delivery to 138 Squadron. In October 1956, Valiants from 138, 148 and 214 squadrons based in Luqa, Malta, saw action in the Suez campaign, becoming the first V bomber to drop bombs in anger. In early 1964, along with other V bombers, the Valiant's role was changed to that of low-level operations. From early 1959, Valiants configured as flight refuelling tankers were delivered to 214 Squadron at Marham, while 543 Squadron at Wyton were equipped with B(PR)K.MK.1s combining the tanker and reconnaissance roles. Valiants were also used in trials of Britain's nuclear weapons.

With about 50 Valiants still in service, fatigue cracks were found in the main wing spars that were deemed uneconomical to repair. The aircraft was grounded in October 1964 before being withdrawn from service in January 1965. The major effect of having the Valiant out of service was to leave the RAF short of an

With the Valiants grounded due to structural problems on 1 January 1965, a few examples had been adapted to the low-level role with the white overall finish altered to that of camouflaged top surfaces. Valiant BK.1 XD818 is seen at the Biggin Hill Battle of Britain display on 19 September 1964 and is now the sole survivor and part of the Cold War Experience at the RAF Museum at Cosford. (*Philip Birtles photo*)

RIGHT: Valiant BK.1 XD816 served as a flight refuelling tanker with 214 Squadron, and, on retirement of the type from RAF service, was allocated to BAC for test flying investigation of structural metal fatigue. Even though the type had been retired from service for over three years, it appeared at the Royal Review of the RAF at Abingdon on 14 June 1968. Although it was a good candidate for preservation, it never flew again and was struck off charge on 26 August 1970, having been scrapped on site. (*Philip Birtles photo*)

LEFT: 543 Squadron operated photo reconnaissance variants of the Valiant, B(PR)1 WZ396 being an example at Wyton in May 1964. They were retired and replaced by Victor SR.2s This aircraft made a wheels up landing at Manston on 23 May 1964. (*Philip Birtles photo*)

air-to-air refuelling capability before the Victor Mk.1s could be converted to the role. One Valiant has been preserved and is housed in the Cold War Experience at Cosford, Shropshire.

The Avro 698 Vulcan was the first to be designed to the full requirements of Specification B.35/46. The delta wing provided a strong structure in which plenty of fuel could be carried and was preceded by five reduced scale Avro 707 experimental aircraft to help prove the concept, although the basic Vulcan was well advanced in construction when these aircraft began flight trials.

The Handley Page HP80 Victor was the second aircraft to be produced which met the requirements of B.35/46. Operated by a crew of five, the Victor's pilot and co-pilot were able to escape in an emergency via ejector seats whereas the remaining crew – two navigators, bomb aimer and radio communications and counter measures operator – used the crew entry door. The distinctive features of the Victor were its crescent wing mounted high on the fuselage and the high-mounted crescent tailplane on a swept back wing. The Victor's crescent wing design was of a tapered sweepback, the thickness of the wing being reduced from the root where the intakes for the Armstrong Siddeley Sapphire engines were situated to a thinner wing tip.

A scale HP.88 research aircraft was built by Blackburn Aircraft which mounted an example of the crescent wing onto a Swift fuselage. The aircraft first flew on 21 June 1951 but was short-lived as it broke up in mid-air at Stansted on 26 August killing the pilot. Two Victor prototypes were built with the first flying at Boscombe Down on 24 December 1952 after being moved by road as a heavily disguised load. Victor production in Radlett consisted of 25 B.MK.1s, 25 of the improved B.1As, 34 Rolls-Royce Conway powered B.Mk.2s; 32 B.Mk.2s were cancelled before being built. To underline the risk of such an advanced structure, the first prototype marked WB771, crashed at Cranfield when the tailplane separated due to flutter while flying low-level position error flights. The Victor entered service with 232 OCU on 28 November 1957, followed by 10 Squadron on 9 April 1958. The first production aircraft, XA917, accidentally exceeded the speed of sound on 1 June 1957 during a test flight. The Mk.1 Victors served with 10, 15, 55 and 57 Squadrons with eight B(PR)1s replacing Valiants with 543 Squadron at Wyton. With the demise of the Valiant, 25 Victor Mk.1s were converted to the tanker configuration

initially as a two-point flight refueller with pods under the wings. Three-point tankers with an additional hose and drogue under the rear fuselage were adopted, the first conversion flying on 2 November 1965 and serving with 55 and 57 Squadrons at Marham, Norfolk.

To further confirm the risks taken on these advanced bombers, prototype Victor B.Mk.2 was lost over the Irish Sea on 20 August 1959 only six months after its first flight while in service with the A&AEE at Boscombe Down – another case of structural failure. The more effective B.Mk.2s could carry the Avro Blue Steel standoff missile which was partly recessed in the bomb bay and operated in the low-level row for which the original white overall paint scheme was changed to that of camouflage. The first unit to receive the improved aircraft was 139 Squadron at Wittering on 1 February 1962, followed by

Valiants of 214 Squadron being broken up at RAF Marham in early 1965, following their withdrawal from service. (*Philip Birtles photo*)

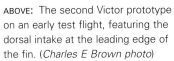

ABOVE: The second Victor prototype on an early test flight, featuring the dorsal intake at the leading edge of the fin. (*Charles E Brown photo*)

ABOVE RIGHT: An early production Victor B.Mk.1 showing the unique wing planform, repeated in the high tail-plane. This aircraft is fitted with a flight refuelling probe over the cockpit and fixed underwing tanks for increased endurance. The aircraft features the overall reflective white finish for protection against the effect of nuclear flash when the aircraft approached its target from high altitude. (*Charles E Brown photo*)

100 Squadron which was located at the same base. With the withdrawal of the Victors as a nuclear deterrent, 100 Squadron was disbanded on 30 September 1968, followed by 139 Squadron on 30 December. The aircraft were ferried to Radlett for Handley Page to undertake conversion to flight refuelling tankers, but when the company went into liquidation in February 1970, the responsibility for the conversation programme was passed to Hawker Siddeley Aviation at Woodford where the Vulcans had been built. The aircraft were flown to Woodford between 25 March and 10 July 1970 where they were modified as tankers, the first 29 conversions being delivered to 232 OCU at Marham on 8 May 1974 for service, and to 214 Squadron which was also based at Marham. These aircraft remained in service and were to support the Vulcan Black Buck operations during the Falklands conflict in 1982

and the Gulf War in 1991, to be withdrawn from service when 55 Squadron disbanded at Marham on 15 October 1993 having completed 39 years of operations.

Another response to the original B.35/46 specification came from de Havilland in the shape of the DH.111 which was based on the Comet 1 and proposed in May 1958. While it did not meet the specification in every respect, it would have provided a low risk interim aircraft. Although not adopted and a further development on the Comet, the Nimrod maritime patrol aircraft is now being converted to the MR.4, and if configured with suitable weapons as has been suggested, could become Britain's future strategic bomber some 25 years after the retirement of the V force. The MR.4 has the load capability and range and is certainly capable of low-level attack as has been demonstrated in its current role.

ABOVE: Photo reconnaissance Victor SR.2 XH672 of 543 Squadron at RAF Wyton after replacing the Valiant. (*Philip Birtles photo*)

RIGHT: Following their replacement by the B.Mk.2s, Victor B.Mk.1s were converted to flight refuelling tankers with hose and drogue units under each wing. Victor BK.1 XA918 is seen here refuelling a pair of Lightning F.2s of 19 Squadron. (*MOD photo*)

Victor BK.1 XA939 of 214 Squadron at
RAF Wattisham in September 1972
complete with camouflage finish for
low-level operations.
(*Philip Birtles photo*)

Early Models

Using data recovered by the Allies from Germany, including some ideas from Walter Lippisch, the delta wing layout was studied by Bob Lindley in the Avro design office. After some thought by Roy Chadwick on his return from illness, the delta layout was adopted for the Vulcan with a number of layouts studied, including winglets (now being developed for more efficient performance on modern airliners) and a central single fin, the latter being chosen. This series of models investigated the layout of the engines and bomb load. Crew accommodation was investigated and attempts were made to feature a jettisonable crew compartment in the event of an emergency. (*BAE Woodford*)

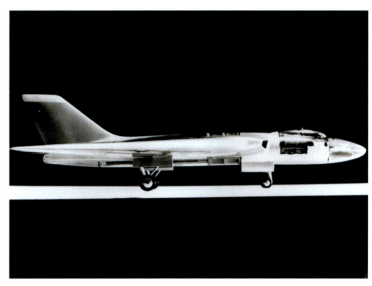

The configuration of the bomb was based on the 10-ton 'Grand Slam' used during the latter part of WW2, but was lighter at 10,000lb and with a length of around 25 feet. The proposed explosive power would be 22 kilotons, similar to the atomic bomb that was dropped on Nagasaki, but the shape would be more streamlined.

For high speed testing, Avro 707A WD280 was fitted with traditional wing route air intakes, similar to the full-scale Vulcan. By this time the configuration of the Vulcan had already been established, but WD280 did identify the need for modifications to the Vulcan wing leading edges, the shape of which was tested on this aircraft. Roly Falk made the maiden flight on 14 July 1951 from Boscombe Down. Following its development programme in Britain, WD280 was shipped to Australia in the spring of 1956 for low-speed testing at Fishermans Bend until 1961. It was retired in February 1967 and acquired by an enthusiast in Williamstown before final preservation at the RAAF Museum at Point Cook from 17 April 1999. (*Avro photo*)

Based on Operational Requirement 229, Specification B.35/46 was issued by the Ministry of Supply (MOS) on 7 January 1947 calling for a strategic bomber to a very demanding standard. It was to be capable of carrying a bomb load of 10,000lb over an air range of 3,350 nautical miles at 500 knots with a maximum ceiling of 50,000 ft. Over shorter ranges, the ordnance would consist of 20,000lb in a weapons bay of 25 ft in length by 5 ft in diameter. The five-man crew was to be accommodated in a pressure cabin that could be jettisoned in an emergency and maintained at 9lb/square inch during cruise flight at 45,000 ft, reduced to 3.5lb/square inch over the target to reduce the risk of an explosive decompression in the event of damage.

Although the British Government had co-operated with the Americans during World War 2 on the joint development of atomic weapon research, the US McMahon Act of August 1946 forbade the release of nuclear information to other nations, including Britain. Fortunately, Britain had access to uranium and had been working with the Canadians, whose own work was independent from the USA. The Joint Chiefs of Staff recommended in October 1945 that Britain should begin to develop an independent nuclear weapon, a notion that was approved by the British Government in January 1947. The configuration of the bomb was based on the 10-ton 'Grand Slam' used during the latter part of WW2, but was lighter at 10,000lb and with a length of around 25 feet. The proposed explosive power would be 22 kilotons, similar to the atomic bomb that was dropped on Nagasaki, but the shape would be more streamlined.

Only two days after the publication of Spec. B.35/46, a number of companies were invited to submit tenders, including A V Roe who had a small team studying a series of designs to meet the requirements of OR229. Roy Chadwick, designer of the wartime Lancaster, had been appointed as the technical director of Avro. During the tender design conference on 28 July 1947, competition was narrowed down to submissions from Avro and Handley Page. At the time of the initial design, Roy Chadwick was sick with shingles; the layout was created by Bob Lindley who led the team to achieve the operational requirement in 1947. Layouts considered were with and without tail sections; the first preliminary study concluded that a wing platform with an aspect lift-to-drag ratio of less than four was necessary. The demands of the specification called for radical thinking with the inclusion of a swept back wing, but there were problems with the structural weight being too high. When scaled down to achieve the required weight and performance, there was insufficient space for its payload and fuel to meet its desired range. Where a swept wing layout appeared impracticable, an all-wing design did have its merits.

Lindley and his designers presumed that a lower aspect ratio of 2.4 was preferable, inevitably of a delta-wing configuration, and more elaborate checks and studies were conducted. The design evolved into a delta layout and eliminated the additional weight of a tail assembly with the required structural strength and accommodation for the engines, undercarriage and fuel buried within the wing. Also, there was adequate space to contain the weapons load although the original design for the aircraft was a long way from what was to become the Vulcan. When the first drawings were completed, Chadwick had recovered from his illness and returned to work. He was surprised to note that the new layout had changed considerably from his original plans, which amounted to little more than a jet-powered Lincoln. His initial doubts as to the new design were expressed rather forcibly, prompting a dispirited Lindley to head home for the weekend. However, by Monday morning, Chadwick had seen the advantages of the delta-wing layout and was enthused, doing much to make it a practical aeroplane (Chadwick was tragically killed less than a month later when Tudor 2 G-AGSU crashed at Woodford on 23 August due to the aileron controls being reversed). During this early period, five Avons or Sapphires powered the aircraft, but in the interests of simplicity, ultimately opted for two engines providing 20,000lb of thrust each. The design team had then heard positive feedback on the new Olympus engine and a four-engine version was promoted for the company brochure, the first of which was published in April 1947. Bob Lindley left for Canada in 1949, joining Avro Aircraft Limited to work on the doomed Avro Arrow delta-wing interceptor, which to this day is the subject of controversy.

Any doubts caused by the loss of Chadwick and the Tudor crew were dispelled by the appointment of William Farren as technical director. Farren had a solid reputation, having served as a former director of the RAE at Farnborough. His efforts contributed to the decision of the MOS to accept the Avro tender on 27 November 1947, a week after a prototype contract had been awarded to Handley Page for the HP.80. An instruction to proceed (ITP) with two prototypes of the Avro

698 was issued on 1 January 1948. By this time, the design had evolved with the engines located side-by-side in the wing roots and the weapons bay to be in a ventral fairing under the wing centreline. For the first time, a forward fuselage was featured housing the crew compartment and radar ahead of the wing. Control was to be maintained from wing trailing edge elevators and ailerons and a conventionally placed fin and rudder mounted on the rear fuselage.

With the basic structural design close to completion in September 1948, there was concern that there was no practical flight information available on the characteristics of a pure delta aircraft. Small-scale research aircraft were required to test the planned flight envelope and Spec E.15/48 was written around the first plane, the Rolls-Royce Derwent powered Avro 707 VX784, construction of which commenced in the summer of 1948 and was completed in August 1949 ready for engine runs and taxiing trials. The aircraft was to test low-speed behaviour

A.V.ROE E15/48
(PROTOTYPE)
DERWENT.
AUGUST 1949.

ABOVE: The prototype Avro 707 VX784 was first flown from Boscombe Down on 4 September 1949 by Eric Esler to test the aerodynamics of the delta wing concept. After appearing statically at the Farnborough Air Show in September 1949, it started the research programme, which was tragically cut short by the fatal crash on 30 September the same year. (*BAE Woodford*)

RIGHT: A second 707A WZ736 was built at Bracebridge Heath near Lincoln, and on completion was towed by road to nearby Waddington where it was flown for the first time on 20 May 1953. This aircraft was ordered for trials with the RAE for pure aerodynamic research and operated from RAE Bedford on the Aero Flight. The test work included development of auto throttles to compensate for the large drag rise from a delta wing at high incidence. WZ736 was withdrawn from use as 7868M on 7 December 1964 and was retired to the Colerne Museum in 1966. The aircraft was found in a dump in early 1967 but was rescued and moved to the collection at Finningley before full restoration and allocation to the Museum of Science and Industry in Manchester on 8 September 1982.
(*Philip Birtles photo*)

RIGHT: Avro 707C WZ744 was a two-seat side-by-side trainer version intended for the possible training of Vulcan pilots in the characteristics of operating delta wing aircraft – it was not adopted. It was assembled at Bracebridge Heath near Lincoln and towed along the road to Waddington where it took to the air for the first time on 1 July 1953. The aircraft was allocated to RAE Farnborough from 1958 for fly-by-wire research until 1967, where it was later allocated as 7932M to the collections at Colerne, Finningley and Topcliffe. It was finally delivered for preservation to Cosford on 13 April 1973 where it is now part of the RAF Museum collection. (*Avro mono & Philip Birtles photo*)

and had a dorsal air intake for the engine, leaving an aerodynamically clean delta wing.

It was transported from Woodford to Boscombe Down for its first flight which was made on 4 September 1949, followed by a static display for the Society of British Aerospace Companies (SBAC) at Farnborough. The aircraft handled well and returned to Boscombe Down for the installation of data measuring equipment after which flight trials were resumed. However, on 30 September, the aircraft crashed near Blackbushe resulting in the death of Eric Esler, Avro's deputy chief test pilot. Although the cause of the crash was never fully established, it was certainly not due to the delta configuration.

A second low-speed 707B prototype, VX790, was constructed with improvements to the controls and had incorporated an ejector seat. VX790 was completed and taken to Boscombe Down in August 1950 where Wing Commander "Roly" Falk, chief test pilot at Avro, made its maiden flight on 6 September, followed by a static appearance at Farnborough. The high-speed 707A WD280 built to Specification E.10/49 made its maiden flight from Boscombe Down on 14 July 1951, by which time construction of the first of two Avro 698 prototypes had already begun. The only direct benefit to the full scale programme was that 707A was found to vibrate significantly at high speed and altitude which was cured by a wing leading edge extension, resulting in the replacement of the leading edges on the first 16 Avro 698 aircraft. Two more 707s were built: 707A WZ736 flying on 20 May 1953, used by the RAE for auto-throttle development, and 707C WZ744 as a planned two-seat side-by-side trainer making its first flight on 1 July 1953 (used by the RAE for systems and power control development).

The large delta wing of the 698 prototype was constructed at Woodford in 1951, with other parts of the airframe built at Chadderton, and moved to final assembly by road. At this late stage in development, the proposed 11,000lb Bristol BE.10 engines proved to be unsatisfactory and were replaced by the Olympus, requiring protracted ground runs into the spring of 1952. Avro were therefore forced to substitute the 6,500lb thrust Rolls-Royce Avon RA.3 to power the 698 prototypes instead. The pressure was on to have the new prototype ready for the SBAC display at Farnborough in September 1952 and hopefully beat the competing HP.80 into the air.

In August the MOS issued contracts to both Avro and Handley Page for initial batches of 25 aircraft of both types. In the last week of August 1952, the overall glossy white delta VX770 rolled out at Woodford and took to the air for the first time in the hands of Roly Falk on 30 August 1952. It had taken 28 months to produce this revolutionary design, despite some delays caused by redesign. After the qualifying flying hours were achieved, the prototype was flown to Boscombe Down on 1 September, from where, due to security reasons, it was displayed over Farnborough accompanied by the all red 707A and the all blue 707B in formation.

Following its appearance at Farnborough, the Vulcan was grounded to have a number of necessary modifications embodied, including the installation of a second ejector seat and cockpit

Vulcan wing and fuselage centre sections as well as other assemblies were built at Chadderton in Manchester. Wings were built at Woodford as they would have been too large to transport by road. The final assembly was at Woodford where test flying was conducted from the airfield. The Olympus engines are in the foreground.
(*Avro photo via Harry Holmes*)

ABOVE: Avro Vulcan first prototype VX770 showing the classic delta wing planform used during the early flight trials. This was an aerodynamic prototype and was initially flown as a single pilot aeroplane without operational equipment fitted. It was later used for engine development work. (*Avro photo*)

RIGHT: First prototype of the Avro Vulcan VX770 on the runway at Farnborough in September 1953, waiting its turn for take-off following the Fairey Gannet overhead. This aircraft made its maiden flight on 30 August 1952 powered by four Rolls-Royce RA-3 Avon engines developing 6,500lb thrust. In 1953, it was converted to four 7,500lb thrust AS.Sa.6 Sapphire engines. It was delivered to R-R at Hucknall on 24 August 1957 for Conway engine development, but crashed at the Syerston Battle of Britain display on 20 September 1958 when it broke up in the air, killing the crew. (*de Havilland photo*)

pressurisation. The original concept of a nosecone that could be jettisoned had been abandoned in favour of equipping the two pilots with ejector seats. The remaining crewmembers – two navigators and an air electronics officer – had to exit the aircraft through the entry hatch which was located in front of the nose wheel undercarriage: a hazard if lowered during an emergency.

The Vulcan returned to the air at the end of October and handling and system tests were undertaken on the limited power of the Avon engines. In May 1953, VX770 was fitted with 7,500lb Sapphire 6 turbojets to start the interim high-speed and high altitude trials. Meanwhile, the second prototype Vulcan VX777 was nearing completion at Woodford and was powered by the long-awaited Olympus engines developing 9,750lb of thrust, ready for its first flight on 3 September 1953. VX777 was accompanied by the first Vulcan prototype and four 707s in a

spectacular formation over Farnborough that week.

The second prototype was designated to high-altitude trials with full pressurisation and to conduct navigation and bombing development. For bombing trials, the Vulcan was fitted with an advanced version of the wartime HS2 radar that kept a constant check on position, track and groundspeed of the aircraft, allowing automatic control in the final approach to the target and release of the weapon.

Although VX777 was delivered to Boscombe Down immediately after its performance at the Farnborough airshow, further trials were delayed due to problems with the installation of the Olympus engines as well as the pressurisation and radar systems. It was not until the spring of 1954 that it was possible to commence with the planned system trials, and these were delayed yet again when VX777 was severely damaged in a heavy

The second prototype Vulcan VX777 which first flew from Woodford on 3 September 1953 powered by four Bristol Olympus 100 engines developing 9,500lb of thrust – later to be Olympus 102 engines that developed 12,000lb. In October 1955, the wing planform was changed to the production shape, and on 31 August 1957 was flown with the new strengthened B.Mk.2 wing and toed-out jet pipes. The last flight of VX777 was to Farnborough on 27 April 1960 where it was used for ground tests before being broken-up in July 1963. (*Avro photo*)

The first production Vulcan B.Mk.1 XA889 originally flew with the straight wing leading edge on 4 February 1955, but later converted to the Phase 2 wing configuration. It was mainly used by Avro for flight development and was powered by progressively more powerful engines starting with 9,750lb thrust Olympus 100 and ending with the 13,400lb thrust Olympus 104 in July 1957. It was delivered to the A&AEE at Boscombe Down in 1967 and withdrawn from use in 1971. (*Avro photo*)

landing at Farnborough. On 30 September 1954, 37 more Vulcans were ordered which were built to an improved B.Mk.1A standard with electronic countermeasures in the tail cone. As had been found with the testing of the 707A WD280, the Vulcan suffered from severe buffet at speeds of over 0.80M – the airflow was separating from the upper surfaces on the outer wing sections causing a compressibility stall, imposing limitations on range, altitude and evasive manoeuvres. The problem was solved by fitting the Phase Two Wing with increased wing sweep outboard and a compensating reduced sweepback to mid span.

The demonstration of Vulcan XA890 by Roly Falk at the 1955 SBAC display showed the aircraft's high manoeuvrability by performing an upward roll, a requirement of the delivery by

low altitude bomber (LABS) of an atomic weapon that allowed it to be well clear of an explosion. The flight deck was similar to that of a jet fighter with a pistol grip control column for better handling. However, the view from the cockpit was minimal due to its construction for canopy strength and crew protection from nuclear flash. The first production Vulcan B.1 XA889 was powered by 10,000lb Olympus 100 engines and flew for the first time on 4 February 1955, to be joined a few days later by VX777 which had been repaired to flying condition. Using XA889 at Boscombe Down, the Vulcan was cleared for service with the RAF on 29 May 1956 which allowed the first delivery of XA897 to 230 OCU at Waddington on 20 July 1956, later to be replaced by XA895.

While 230 OCU was starting its training programmes, Vulcan XA897 had been returned to Woodford for preparation for its first overseas flight as a diplomatic exercise to New Zealand via Australia. The outbound flight was trouble-free and among the crew was Air Marshal Sir Harry Broadhurst, C-in-C Bomber Command who shared the flying duties with the captain, Squadron Leader Donald Howard. On the final leg of the return flight, a departure was made from Aden on 1 October 1956 with Heathrow as the destination, where a reception committee was waiting to welcome the crew. Following a radio call *en route*, the weather forecast was predicted as having a cloud base at 700ft with heavy rain and a visibility at 300ft of 1000 yards. Normal air traffic was experiencing no problems with landings and the Vulcan approached the runway with the assistance of ground-controlled approach (GCA). The first sign of the aircraft from the ground was a brief sound of power with the Vulcan climbing steeply up to 500ft when the two pilots were seen to eject, the aircraft going into a shallow dive before crashing into the ground, killing the four crew in the rear. The resulting enquiries found that the aircraft had impacted with the ground in the undershoot some 1000 yards from the touchdown point, removing both main undercarriage legs and damaging the elevator controls which explained why the Vulcan climbed steeply until the pilots realised that all control had been lost. The subsequent RAF Court of Enquiry found that the principal cause of the accident was the failure of the GCA controller to warn the captain that the aircraft was going below the glide path, although the controller was not held to blame.

LEFT: Avro 707B VX790 was produced to the same specification as VX784, but had a longer nose and the modified cockpit. Construction was monocoque and a modified Sea Hawk nose leg gave better angle of incidence on take-off. Its first flight was by Roly Falk on 6 September 1950. Following completion of the test programme, VX790 went to the Empire Test Pilots School at Farnborough, but was grounded after a landing accident on 25 September 1956. It was transferred to RAE Bedford for spares recovery and was scrapped in 1960. (*Charles E Brown photo*)

BELOW: Avro 707B VX790 was fitted with a dorsal air intake for the Rolls-Royce Derwent turbojet engine, providing a pure delta wing for aerodynamic development. Its first public appearance was at the Farnborough Air Show soon after the first flight, following which the development programme commenced at Boscombe Down. (*BAE Heritage Centre photo*)

RIGHT: Avro 707A WD280 which was more similar in layout to the planned Vulcan bomber with air intakes for the Rolls-Royce Derwent jet engine in the wing root. This aircraft made its first flight from Boscombe Down on 14 July 1951 and following its test programmes was shipped to Australia in 1956, where after further test flying it was preserved.
(*BAE Heritage Centre photo*)

LEFT: Avro 707A WD280 was used to test the new aerodynamic shape of the proposed Phase 2 wing leading edge before its adoption on the Vulcan.
(*BAE Heritage Centre photo*)

ABOVE: Avro 707A WZ736 which made its maiden flight from Boscombe Down on 20 May 1953. It was based at the RAE Farnborough, and amongst the test flying work was auto-throttle development. It is now preserved in the Manchester Museum of Science and Industry.
(*BAE Heritage Centre photo*)

LEFT: For the 1953 Farnborough Air Show, Avro flew a formation of the two Vulcan prototypes, flanked by the two 707As, the 707B and the two-seat 707C (*BAE Woodford*)

LEFT: Avro Vulcan prototype VX770 showing the original straight wing leading edge configuration. (*BAE Heritage Centre photo*)

BELOW: The Prototype Vulcan VX770 taxiing out for its maiden flight from Woodford on 30 August 1952. (*BAE Heritage Centre photo*)

BELOW: The Prototype Vulcan VX770 landing at Woodford following its maiden flight by Roly Falk on 30 August 1952. Not only are the wing mounted airbrakes deployed, but also the brake parachute to slow down the aircraft and save wear and tear on the brakes. (*BAE Heritage Centre photo*)

RIGHT: The first prototype Vulcan VX770 rolled out of the Woodford factory for the first time after completion. Alongside is an Avro Ashton jet research aircraft. (*BAE Woodford*)

SEQUENCE BELOW: The Vulcan prototype VX770 made its maiden flight from the Avro airfield at Woodford on 30 August 1952. (*BAE Woodford*)

LEFT: The Vulcan Prototype VX770 displayed at the Farnborough air show in 1952.
(*RAF Museum photo*)

BELOW: The Vulcan wing centre section and fuselage were built as an integral unit at the Avro factory in Manchester. They were then moved by road to the Woodford site for final assembly. The journey between the two sites had to be carefully planned and this bridge was probably the tightest access with only 18 inches clearance to spare on either side. Some street lamp supports also had to be hinged to fold back out of the way. (*BAE Woodford*)

LEFT: Production of the Vulcan fuselage and stub wing assembly was undertaken at the vast facility at Chadderton in Manchester. This factory has recently been demolished and the site cleared. (*BAE Woodford*)

BELOW AND RIGHT: Vulcan stub wing and fuselage centre section assembly line at the Avro factory at Chadderton, Manchester. (*BAE Heritage Centre photo*)

BELOW: The nose sections including the flight decks were built at the Avro Chadderton factory and shipped to Woodford for final assembly followed by flight testing. (*BAE Woodford*)

RIGHT: Final assembly of the Vulcan V-Bombers was undertaken at the Woodford factory where Lancaster bombers were built during World War 2. (*BAE Heritage Centre photo*)

Third production Vulcan B.1 XA891 flew initially with the straight wing leading edge but was later modified to the Phase 2 standard. It was used by Avro for development and powered by 16,000lb thrust Olympus 200 engines as later fitted to Vulcan Mk.2s. This aircraft crashed at Walkington, Yorks, on 24 July 1959, the crew surviving. (*Avro photo*)

The second prototype Vulcan VX777 was used to test the full scale aerodynamics of the modified wing leading edge, later adopted for all production aircraft. (*BAE Woodford*)

ABOVE: Vulcan Mk.1 XA892 served briefly with 230 OCU before being delivered to Farnborough for ballistics research. It was retired to RAF Halton on 21 June 1962, landing on the short grass airfield where it became 7746M, still retaining its overall silver finish. It was used by apprentices for engine running and systems checking until it was scrapped in July 1971. (*Philip Birtles photo*)

RIGHT: A rare colour image of an early production Vulcan B.1 XA895 in the early silver finish, later replaced by overall white. (*BAE Woodford*)

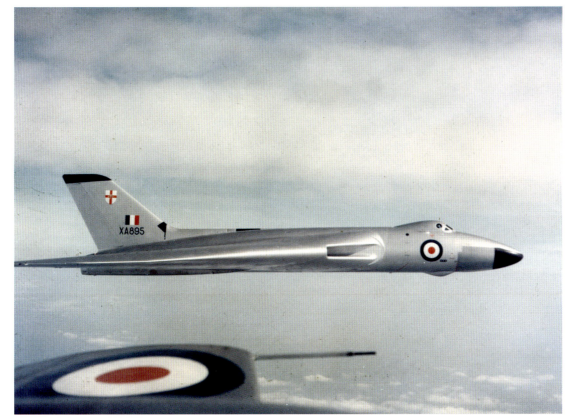

ABOVE: Vulcan Mk.1 XA900 was operated by 230 OCU from 25 March 1957, 101 Squadron and then returned to 230 OCU. During its first period with 230 OCU it was flown by HRH The Duke of Edinburgh on 24 June 1958. It was retired to Cosford on 19 November 1965 as 7896M for technical training, joining the Aerospace Museum collection by 1979 when it was the only surviving Vulcan Mk.1. However, as there was nowhere to keep it under cover, it had to be scrapped due to corrosion. It was replaced by B.Mk.2 XM598 on 21 January 1983, which had been allocated for Black Buck operations. (*Philip Birtles photo*)

Some of the early Vulcan Mk.1s were allocated to development flying and never entered operational service. XA903 was an example, which was used for Blue Steel development before becoming an engine test-bed with Rolls-Royce at Filton. It was initially used to test the Concorde Olympus engine, mounted in a representative nacelle under the bomb bay. It was then fitted with a pod for the Turbo Union RB.199 engine for the Tornado. It made its final flight from Filton to Farnborough on 22 February 1979, which was also the final flight of a Vulcan Mk.1. (*RAE photo*)

ABOVE: The hard worked Vulcan B.1 XA903 development aircraft was allocated to engine test-bed work with Bristol Siddeley Engines at Filton. It was initially allocated to Concorde Olympus flight testing and had a water-spray rig mounted in front of the engine to test the effects of severe icing. (*RAF Museum photo*)

LEFT: The Vulcan B.1 XA903 engine test-bed was also used to assist in the flight development programme for the Turbo-Union RB199 engine which powers the Tornado fleets for the air forces of Britain, Europe and Saudi Arabia. (*RAF Museum photo*)

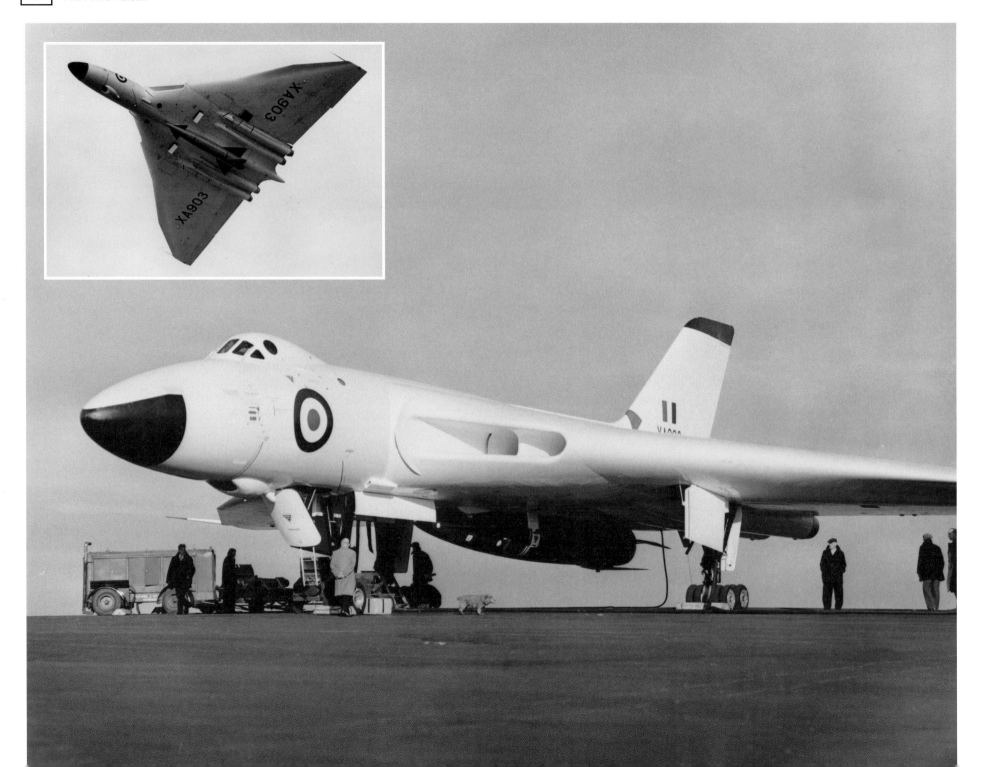

LEFT: Vulcan Mk.1 XA903 was the Blue Steel development aircraft with Avro at Woodford, first showed publicly in September 1958 with a Blue Steel missile slung under the bomb bay. (*Avro photo*)

INSET LEFT: Test Vulcan B.1 XA903 was used for Blue Steel stand-off missile trials, with the weapon located in recessed doors under the bomb bay. (*RAF Museum photo*)

INSET: The first production Vulcan B.Mk.2 was XH533 with more powerful Olympus engines and a larger wing, and made its first flight from Woodford on 19 August 1958. This aircraft was not fitted with the ECM tail-cone. Following the manufacturer's trial, the XH533 was used for automatic landing trials at Woodford and the RAE. It was broken up at 19 MU St Athan in 1970. (*Avro photo*)

RIGHT: Vulcan B.2 XH535 was allocated to the A&AEE at Boscombe Down for service trials, but crashed near Andover 11 May 1964 after loss of control. The two pilots were able to eject, but the four crew members in the rear were killed.
(*HSA photo*)

RIGHT: Vulcan B.2 XH537 was the Douglas Skybolt development aircraft, the large cruise missile being carried under each wing on pylons. Many of the production Vulcan B.Mk.2s featured the structural strengthening in the wing for the pylons, which later was to prove useful hard points for other weapon systems. The first of four dummy Skybolt releases were made over the West Freugh Ranges in Scotland on 1 December 1961. (*Avro photo*)

LEFT: The first flight of Vulcan XH537 carrying dummy Skybolt missiles was from Woodford on 29 September 1961. This aircraft later served with 230 OCU at Finningley and Scampton and was converted to a MR.2 configuration from April 1974 at Bitteswell and delivered to 27 Squadron 18 June 1974. (*Avro photo*)

RIGHT: Vulcan B.Mk.2 XH539 was used for Blue Steel low-level trials from Edinburgh Field in Australia while serving with the A&AEE. It was finally flown to Waddington on 7 March 1972 where it was used for fire training. (*Philip Birtles photo*)

LEFT: The first production Vulcan B.Mk.2 was XH558 which made its first flight from Woodford on 25 May 1960. Its last flight was 20 September 1992 and is currently under restoration to airworthiness. (BAE Heritage Centre photo)

ABOVE: Vulcan B.2 XM603 was returned to its home at Woodford on 12 March 1982. This aircraft was maintained in working order by a group of volunteers. It was finally declared unsafe in late 2006, following which it was used for spares for the Vulcan at Bruntingthorpe. (*BAE Heritage Centre photo*)

With the development of British megaton standard weapons for the second generation V-Bombers, the aircraft would approach its target, and after releasing its payload, make a tight 180 degree turn to avoid the effects of the blast, as well as the Soviet missile defences, which by the end of 1960 had a range of 25 miles up to an altitude of 60,000 feet.

Vulcan B.Mk.2 XH558 at Goose Bay in the typical winter surroundings. It would have just been pushed out of the heated hangar and the daily inspection started ready for a low-level sortie over the barren wastes of Canada, which provided a realistic environment of typical approaches to Siberia. (*MOD photo*)

From the end of May 1957, the strength of 230 OCU increased to train sufficient crews to join frontline squadrons. Pilots and co-pilots came from Canberra units who were highly experienced in flying jets at high altitudes and speeds, as did the majority of the navigators who also served with Canberra squadrons. The pilots flew around fifty hours at the OCU and were joined by the navigators and Air Electronic Officer (AEO). The first operational Vulcans graduated on 20 May 1957 at Waddington to form A Flight of 83 Squadron, the first aircraft received by the unit on 11 July with a total of six bombers being delivered before the end of the year, allowing intensive training and overseas flights, including participating in the annual USAF Strategic Air Command Bombing, Navigation and Reconnaissance Competition. The RAF Valiants, with their more experienced crews, beat the Vulcans with 214 Squadron achieving 11th place out of 90 competitors, the majority on their home territory. Other overseas tours included Africa and South America.

The Vulcan force continued to grow with 101 Squadron reforming at Finningley on 15 October 1957, two weeks after taking delivery of their first aircraft, with seven more added by the end of April 1958. This was followed by the famous 'Dam Busters', 617 Squadron at Scampton which reformed on 1 May 1958. Their first aircraft were delivered on 5 May, the full compliment of eight Vulcan B.Mk1As following by mid-November.

As experience increased, the Vulcan squadrons operated a number of overseas flights to build on navigational accuracy and were often self-supporting with spares and baggage carried in a pannier in the bomb bay. Australia and New Zealand, as well as parts of Asia, were included in these operations with colder climates being experienced in Norway and Canada. In the 1950s the V-Force, aircraft were dispersed to 36 airfields around Britain, reduced to 26 by 1962. Although some dispersals were pre-planned, many were not, resulting in the crews maintaining cases packed ready for a rapid departure. When an exercise alert was called, the aircrew would report to the Operations Wing while the ground crew would be preparing the aircraft for flight, including a brief ground engine run. The initial Readiness One-Five (fifteen minutes) allowed final checks to be completed before Readiness Zero-Five being called. At Readiness Zero-Two, the Vulcan's engines were started and the aircraft would then be sent to their designated dispersal airfields in groups of four.

The aircraft would then be parked on the Operational Readiness Platform (ORP) beside the duty runway. The crews lived in special caravans alongside their aircraft, allowing a scramble at short notice, the Vulcan having full take-off checks every twenty-four hours. On the call for scramble, the AEO was the first crewmember to climb into the aircraft, turning on the external power needed to start the engines. Once power had been

ABOVE: Vulcan B.Mk.1 XA901 was delivered initially to 230 OCU on 4 April 1957 and joined 83 Squadron on 27 June 1960 as shown here. After returning to 230 OCU, it was delivered the RAF College at Cranwell for technical training on 19 November 1965 as 7897M until scrapped in October 1972. (*Philip Birtles photo*)

ABOVE RIGHT: Vulcan B.1 XA897 of 230 OCU at Changi, Singapore, in September 1956. Following a tour of New Zealand and Australia, this aircraft crashed at London Heathrow in poor weather on 1 October 1956. The four crew in the rear found themselves unable to escape in time and were all killed. (*RAF Museum photo*)

RIGHT: Vulcan B.Mk.1A XA912 in low-level camouflage finish with the Waddington Wing. This was built as a B.Mk.1 and later converted to the B.Mk.1A at Bitteswell which featured ECM equipment located in a modified tail-end of the fuselage. (*Avro photo via Harry Holmes*)

ABOVE: Vulcan B.Mk.1 XH481 of 101 Squadron at Waddington. This aircraft was the holder of the England to Australia record of 9,993 nautical miles in 20 hours 3 minutes on 22 June 1961 achieved by flight refuelling. It was withdrawn from use in 1967 and taken to Cottesmore for fire training on 11 January 1968. (*RAF Museum photo*)

ABOVE RIGHT: Vulcan B.Mk.1A XH483 of 50 Squadron was originally delivered to the RAF on 20 May 1958, serving initially with 617 Squadron and later operated by the Waddington Wing. It was withdrawn from use on 3 August 1967 and allocated to Manston for fire training. (*RAF Museum photo*)

RIGHT: Vulcan B.2s of 9 and 12 Squadrons at readiness on the ORP, probably at Conningsby, with an Anson – an earlier aircraft from the Avro stable – flying overhead. (*RAF Museum photo*)

generated, the pilot, with assistance from the co-pilot, would start the engines, followed by the nav radar and nav plotter who would close the entrance hatch. Within two minutes, the V-Bombers would taxi on to the runway for immediate take-off following each other into the air. Not all war loads consisted of nuclear weapons with some aircraft tasked to carry conventional iron bombs. The standard nuclear weapon of the time was the 10,000lb Blue Danube bomb with strict safeguards in its deployment. The three Vulcan squadrons of No 1 Group assumed the role of spearheading Britain's nuclear deterrent force, supported by three

squadrons of Valiants and three squadrons of Victors: 10, 15 and 57, equipping 3 Group. The last Vulcan B.1 of 45 were built, was delivered to the RAF at the end of March 1959 to be followed by the more capable Vulcan B.Mk.2.

The Vulcan B.Mk.2 had its wing area increased from 3,446 to 3,965 square feet and the wingspan increased from 99 to 111 feet, the aircraft benefiting from the new Olympus 200 engines that developed more power. The new wing, known as the Phase 2C, improved performance at altitude and increased the range by 600 miles. The wing was approved by the MOS in October 1955 and work commenced on the second generation Vulcan with a production order placed in June 1956. The new model of Vulcan saw the end of B.1 production, the last 25 B.1s being replaced by B.2s and a further 24 aircraft added to the deterrent force.

Vulcan prototype VX777 led the aerodynamic programme, flying with the new wing on 31 August 1957, while other Mk.1s were used in other aspects of development testing; XA891 being used as the Olympus 200 test-bed. All of the aerodynamic and systems changes were brought together in XH533, the first production B.Mk.2 which was first flown from Woodford on 19 August 1958, in time for the SBAC Display at Farnborough the following month. Not only did this particular aircraft have a new wing configuration and more powerful Olympus engines with enlarged air intakes, other improvements included a strengthened undercarriage with a shorter nose leg, an auxiliary power unit, a new AC electrical system and new Electronic Counter Measures (ECM) systems were fitted in an enlarged tail-cone.

The first seven B.Mk.2s were used for development before their delivery to the RAF, XH558 being the first to 230 OCU on 1 July 1960. As the new B.2s were delivered, 29 of the remaining 34 B.1s were withdrawn for modification to B.1A standards incorporating the improved ECM systems.

With a significantly increased Vulcan fleet, the opportunity was taken to reorganise its units. The B.1s and B.1As were stationed at Waddington with 44 (Rhodesia) Squadron reforming on 10 August and receiving its first aircraft in January 1961. 230 OCU, which was equipped with both marks of Vulcan, moved to RAF Finningley and the first B.2 course to graduate was posted to 83 Squadron at Scampton in October 1960, receiving its first B.Mk.2 on 23 December. On 1 April 1961, 27 Squadron reformed at Scampton with the first Vulcan B.2 being delivered on 20 April, and 617 Squadron received its first B.2 on 1 September 1961, completing the Scampton Wing.

With increased Vulcan deliveries, a second B.2 wing was formed at Coningsby with IX Squadron reformed on 1 March 1962 as the first unit, taking delivery of its first Vulcan on 11 May. IX Squadron was joined by 12 Squadron on 1 July 1962 and received its first aircraft on 25 September, the Wing being completed with the inclusion of 35 Squadron on 1 December 1962. The Vulcans from Coningsby mainly originated from the Scampton Wing, which was gradually re-equipping its aircraft to carry the Blue Steel standoff weapon. By this time, the Scampton crews were becoming increasingly experienced on the Vulcan B.2 and were involved in a number of major exercises, particularly with the USAF on their home ground. On 14 October 1961, four Vulcans from 27 and 83 Squadrons made successful high-level mock attacks on the USA at 56,000 feet, making good use of their ESM and returned to the UK undetected by the American defences. The V-Force was on its highest state of alert during the Cuban Missile Crisis in October 1962 when the Russians attempted to base their intermediate-range ballistic missile (IRBMs) in Cuba. The V-Bombers were on a high state of readiness in a secure environment and were combat ready for a period of three days.

LEFT: 83 Squadron was the first active unit to receive the Vulcan B.Mk.2s when they were delivered to Scampton in the anti-flash white finish. (*RAF Museum photo*)

RIGHT: Vulcan B.Mk.2s lined up at RAF Scampton in 1981 consisting of MRR XH560 of 27 Squadron, XL445 of 35 Squadron, XM652 of 44 (Rhodesia) Squadron, XL427 of 50 Squadron, XM657 of 44 Squadron in 101 Squadron markings and XL318 of 617 Squadron. (*Bruce Woodruff photo via VRT*)

With the development of British megaton standard weapons for the second generation V-Bombers, the aircraft would approach its target, and after releasing its payload, make a tight 180 degree turn to avoid the effects of the blast, as well as the Soviet missile defences, which by the end of 1960 had a range of 25 miles up to an altitude of 60,000 feet. This was clearly demonstrated when CIA pilot Francis Gary Powers was shot down by a Soviet missile on 1 May 1960 while flying a spy U-2 aircraft at high altitude over the USSR. As a consequence, the V-Force adopted a new tactic by flying low altitude operations to avoid radar detection, and the overall white finish was replaced by camouflaged top surfaces and grey undersides.

RIGHT: Vulcan B.2 XL320 of 230 OCU at Wattisham in September 1972 which was delivered to the RAF on 1 December 1961. It initially served with the Scampton Wing and 27 Squadron and was withdrawn to 19 MU at St Athan on 2 June 1981. (*Philip Birtles photo*)

BELOW: Vulcan B.2 XL392 of 617 Squadron at Abingdon in September 1978, although it is not carrying a Blue Steel. This aircraft was originally delivered to 83 Squadron in August 1962 and was flown from Scampton to RAF Valley on 24 March 1982 for fire fighting training. (*Philip Birtles photo*)

BELOW RIGHT: Vulcan B.2 XL444 of 617 Squadron was in the static display at Greenham Common in July 1976. This aircraft was originally delivered to the RAF on 30 October 1962 and served initially with 27 Squadron and the Scampton Wing. It ended up with the Waddington Wing and was withdrawn from use and scrapped in December 1982. (*Philip Birtles photo*)

ABOVE: Vulcan B.Mk.2 XL321 of 617 Squadron carrying a Blue Steel missile as part of the Scampton Wing in the overall white anti-flash high-level finish before low-level operations were introduced. The Scampton Wing maintained the British nuclear deterrent until it was replaced by Polaris nuclear submarines. (*HSA photo*)

RIGHT: Scampton Wing Vulcan B.2 XL386 at Abingdon in June 1968 for the RAF Jubilee with Blue Steel mounted below the bomb bay. This aircraft made its last flight from Waddington to Manston on 26 August 1982 to be used for training by the Fire School. (*Philip Birtles photo*)

The aircraft were still vulnerable to the Eastern Bloc defences and the Blue Steel standoff weapon was developed, entering service in February 1963.

Development of the Blue Steel nuclear missile began in March 1956 when Avro received a development contract from the MOS and initial flight trials involving ⅔th scale models were launched from a Valiant over Aberporth ranges. The full-scale missile was powered by an Armstrong Siddeley Stentor rocket engine that allowed supersonic cruise speeds, the first representative launch being in mid-1960. The missile was a 'fire-and-forget' system with inertial navigation resulting in it being impossible to be diverted from its target after launch. Blue Steel was designed to be launched from both the Vulcan and Victor, and because of its size, could not be carried

internally in the bomb bay, and was therefore recessed with the lower part of the missile exposed. The first test firing was made at the Woomera rocket range in Australia in early 1961, and the first unit to equip with Blue Steel was 617 Squadron at Scampton in August 1962, being declared fully operational in February 1963.

Operational Blue Steel missiles were only carried by aircraft on a quick reaction alert (QRA), a role where NATO developed a rapid-response attack to counter a sudden Warsaw Pact/Soviet Union nuclear strike. Under hostile conditions, the aircraft would make a steep turn away from the weapon after launch at an altitude of 50,000 feet. The missile would climb to 70,000 feet and accelerate to Mach 2.5 before diving to its target with a range of 100 nautical miles, its accuracy being half a mile from its intended objective and delivering a thermonuclear warhead. Blue Steel could also be launched at low-level at Mach 1.6 with a range of up to 200 nautical miles. Towards the end of 1963, 27 and 83 Squadrons were equipped with Blue Steel at Scampton, as well as 100 and 139 Squadron Victors at Wittering. These aircraft formed the spearhead of Bomber Command's nuclear deterrent with four Vulcans on QRA and airborne within 90 seconds of starting to roll using a mass rapid start of the four engines simultaneously.

While Blue Steel could have been developed into an effective air-launched cruise missile, it was abandoned in favour

ABOVE: Vulcan B.2MR XH537 at Abingdon which served with 27 Squadron. It was rumoured to be destined for preservation, but by September 1982, it had already been robbed of its flight refuelling probe for Black Buck operations and was later scrapped. (*Philip Birtles photo*)

LEFT: Vulcan B.2s XH558 and XH557 flying over RAF Fylingdales radar installation which commenced operation in January 1964 to assist in identifying potential targets, giving advanced warning of an attack to the QRA force. XH558 was the first B.2 to be delivered to the RAF and is the example being restored to flight at Bruntingthorpe. XH557 made its first flight on 19 May 1961 and was initially allocated to Olympus development. Following this it was allocated to the Waddington Wing and scrapped in December 1982. (*MOD photo*)

of fitting Vulcans with the American air-launched Skybolt missile that were stowed on underwing pylons. The Douglas Aircraft Corporation was awarded a design study contract by the US Government in May 1959, followed by a further contract in February 1960 to cover the construction of test vehicles. Skybolt came within the IRBM category and had a range of 1,150 miles and four missiles could be carried on the underwing pylons of a B-52 strategic bomber.

The RAF began to show interest in this advanced system in 1959 as a replacement for Blue Steel, to extend the British airborne nuclear deterrent into the 1970s. An agreement was reached in March 1960 for Skybolt to be supplied to the RAF with a target in service date with the Strategic Air Command (SAC) at the end of 1963. The intention was for Britain to buy an initial batch of 100 Skybolts. Avro was selected as the main British integration contractor for Skybolt with the Vulcan B.2 as the selected carrier, initially with a missile under each wing. As a result, 40 Vulcan B.Mk.2s were fitted with strengthened wing structures and Skybolt attachment points, powered by 20,000lb thrust Olympus 301 engines, later to prove invaluable during Operation Black Buck (see Chapter Four).

In November 1961, Vulcan XH537 flew from Woodford with a pair of dummy Skybolts on wing pylons and made its first release in the UK on 1 December. A joint trials force was set up at Eglin Air Force Base in Florida in 1962 where responsibility for Skybolt trials rested. During the initial trial firings, Skybolt's performance was disappointing, and by the end of 1962, the programme had cost $500 million. The missile programme attracted a review by US Secretary of Defence, Robert McNamara, who recommended on 7 November that the Skybolt project be cancelled, a decision that left the RAF without a weapon to replace Blue Steel. The cancellation was confirmed in December. Offers by President Kennedy to allow Britain to continue development of the Skybolt programme were rejected as too costly and British Prime Minister Harold Macmillan opted for Polaris, a submarine-launched nuclear deterrent in February 1963.

The V-Force was at its peak in mid-1964 with its role altered drastically from high-altitude weapons delivery to low-level air attack. The older Valiants were unable to withstand the additional stresses and were retired from active service after cracks were found in the wings, but the Vulcan was robust enough to undertake the stresses of flight at or below 1000 feet.

In June 1964, the Vulcan B.1/1As were withdrawn from service with the aircraft serving with 230 OCU, leaving it with B.2s. The alteration to low-level operations required the Vulcan crews to undertake a major change in training, the main responsibility for this being assumed by the RAF Bomber Command detachment at Goose Bay in Labrador, Canada, with Vulcans visiting every week of the year. This allowed each crew to fly three low-level routes across the wildest terrain, which was similar to the Arctic regions of the Soviet Union where the V-Force might have to operate in times of tension. Other advantages included the lack of air traffic operating in the area as well as large swathes of unpopulated terrain. The nearest civilian town to Goose Bay was over 700 miles and the airfield was usually cut off during the winter from all surface transport due to ice and snow.

The final Vulcan B.2 was delivered to 35 Squadron in December 1964, and at the same time, the Coningsby Wing (IX, 12 and 35 Squadron) moved to Cottesmore in Rutland. In January 1964, the QRA continued to be maintained with the assistance of the early warning system at Fylingdales in Yorkshire, the Vulcans armed with megaton range standoff or free-fall and conventional weapons. The Vulcan's conventional role was decidedly useful during the Indonesian confrontation in 1963–1965 where, in an agreement with Malaysia, Britain assisted the country's defence against Indonesian insurgents with bombers being based in Tengah, Singapore, and Butterworth in Malaysia. The Vulcans were never used in anger, Hunters and Canberras being used for close air support. The Vulcan operations were known as Sunflower detachments usually consisting of eight aircraft with four Vulcans on standby, two in reserve and two under maintenance. While on these detachments, the opportunity was taken for the Vulcans to visit Darwin for additional realistic training where the ECM could be used with minimum restrictions.

With the merger of Bomber and Fighter Commands into Strike Command on 30 April 1968, the Vulcan force maintained the QRA vanguard, the two Victor B.2 squadrons being disbanded by the end of the year. 12 Squadron had disbanded at Cottesmore on 31 December 1967, its aircraft going to the Waddington Wing which became exclusively equipped with B.2s by January 1968. In January 1969, the two remaining Cottesmore units, IX and 35 Squadrons, left to form the Near East Air Force (NEAF) Bomber Wing at Akrotiri in Cyprus. On 30 June 1969, the Vulcan QRA was withdrawn with the handover of the strategic nuclear deterrent duties to the Royal Navy. The remaining Vulcan force was allocated with the conventional bombing role with free-fall weapons, but could still be tasked for nuclear operations if required. At the time there were seven units equipped with Vulcans: three at Waddington, two at Scampton, two at Akrotiri and 83 Squadron disbanded on 31 August 1969.

The first Vulcan unit to become operational in Akrotiri was 35 Squadron on 15 January 1969, followed by IX Squadron on 26 February. The NEAF responsibility was both national and international with a major contribution to NATO, and was particularly appropriate when El Adem in Libya was vacated by the RAF in March 1970, greatly increasing the Russian influence in the Mediterranean.

The Vulcans contributed to the defence of the Central Treaty Organisation (CENTO) which consisted of Britain, Iran, Turkey, Pakistan with the USA as associates, providing a tactical bombing spearhead if required under RAF control. The Vulcans were deployed on a variety of training profiles, with 35

Squadron undertaking most of the more interesting long-range sorties, while IX Squadron operations tending to be limited to the Middle East. With the Turkish invasion of northern Cyprus in mid-1974, the Bomber Wing was dispersed with many of the aircraft coming to be stationed in Malta. To help diffuse the political situation, the Vulcans were withdrawn from the Mediterranean and returned to Britain, with IX Squadron joining the Waddington Wing and 35 Squadron to Scampton.

The whole of 1 Group Vulcan force assumed the conventional role at the end of 1970 in support of NATO with the Blue Steel missiles of 27 and 617 Squadrons being withdrawn and scrapped. The major weapons were 1000lb retarded bombs with training priority being night operations to enhance survivability in a hostile environment. The Vulcans were now showing their age; they were becoming more difficult to maintain but major overseas exercises were still tasked,

ABOVE: Vulcan B.2 XM605 at Biggin Hill in September 1964 in a view often experienced by airshow crowds. XM605 was delivered to the RAF on 20 December 1963, initially operated by IX Squadron as part of the Cottesmore Wing, before moving to Waddington. It was flown to Castle Air Force Base in California on 8 September 1981 for display at the USAF Museum. (*Philip Birtles photo*)

RIGHT: A familiar view of the Vulcan at airshows with bomb doors open, showing the large bomb bay. 230 OCU aircraft XL388 makes a flypast at Cottesmore in September 1973 and also served with 9 Squadron. This aircraft made its final flight from Waddington to Honington on 2 April 1982 to be used for fire practice. (*Philip Birtles photo*)

BELOW: Waddington Wing Vulcan B.2 XH557 making a fly past at the annual Hatfield open day in July 1973. This aircraft had been used for Olympus research, making its first flight on 19 May 1961 and was scrapped in December 1982. In the background is the Manor Road site with the Blue Streak space rocket tower beyond. (*Philip Birtles photo*)

including round the world flights with Singapore and Australia providing realistic alternative training environments.

On 29 March 1972, 27 Squadron disbanded at Scampton, but reformed at the same base on 1 November 1973 with four Vulcan SR.2s modified for the maritime strategic reconnaissance role, replacing the Victors of 543 Squadron at Wyton. 230 OCU had moved from Finningley towards the end of 1969 to join 27 and 617 Squadrons, with the other four squadrons at Waddington. The crews of the Vulcan force maintained their skills by participating in US based international exercises including 'Giant Voice' and 'Red Flag', where they held their own against home-based competition.

By 1979, it was decided that the Vulcans had reached the end of their operational service and the stripping of the V-Force commenced in December 1980 when XM653 was flown from Waddington to St Athan for scrapping. With the reduced need for conversion training, 230 OCU disbanded in mid-1981, followed by 617 Squadron on 1 January 1982. The other two Scampton based squadrons, 35 and 27 Squadrons, disbanded on 1 March and 31 March respectively. 101 Squadron disbanded at Waddington on 5 August 1982 and 44 Squadron continued to operate the Vulcan until it was disbanded on 27 December 1982 – the last two units having supplied crews and aircraft for operations against the Argentinian forces on the Falklands, giving the Vulcan its first and only combat action in Operation Black Buck (see Chapter 4).

In April 1982, while Operation Corporate (the British counter-invasion of the Falkland Islands) was still underway, a meeting was held at British Aerospace at Woodford to investigate the possibility of converting a number of Vulcans to the tanker role: the aim being to assist the Victors while VC-10s were converted for use in 101 Squadron. On 4 May, six Vulcans were converted, and on 23 June, the first was delivered to 50 Squadron at Waddington when the first successful transfer was made to Victor K.2. The standard hose drum unit was mounted in the tail, replacing the ECM equipment and additional fuel tanks were fitted in the bomb bay. In addition to the six conversions, three more Vulcans were also taken on charge as reserves and for training, making 50 Squadron the last to operate Vulcans. 50 Squadron finally disbanded on 31 March 1984 as 101 Squadron VC-10s joined the RAF tanker fleet.

44 Squadron Vulcan B.2 XJ784 from Waddington at Greenham Common in June 1979. This aircraft had originally been operated by the A&AEE at Boscombe Down before joining 230 OCU. It also served with the NEAF at Akrotiri before joining 44 Squadron, and was scrapped in December 1982. (*Philip Birtles photo*)

Cottesmore Wing Vulcan B.2 XL445 attended the Hatfield open day in July 1968. It was delivered to the RAF on 24 November 1962 and was operated by 27 Squadron, IX Squadron – NEAF, 230 OCU, 35 Squadron and 44 Squadron, finally serving with 50 Squadron as a flight refuelling tanker. (*Philip Birtles photo*)

LEFT: Vulcan B.Mk.2 XM603 of 44 Squadron which was delivered to the RAF on 3 December 1963 and served with the Conningsby and Waddington Wings. It was flown to Woodford, the home of the Vulcan on 12 March 1982, where it was painted overall white and has been maintained in functional condition. (*RAF Museum photo*)

BELOW LEFT: 50 Squadron Vulcan B.2 XL427 lifts off from Waddington in May 1981. It was initially delivered to 83 Squadron at Waddington before leaving for RAF Machrihanish on 13 August 1982 for fire practice training. (*Philip Birtles photo*)

BELOW: Vulcan B.2 XM606 of 27 Squadron with the Union Jack on the fin, demonstrating at the Sao Paulo airshow in September 1973. It was delivered to the RAF on 20 December 1963 and its last flight was to Barksdale AFB in Louisiana on 9 June 1982 for preservation at the 8th Air Force museum. (*Philip Birtles photo*)

Vulcan B.2 XM648 of IX Squadron at Mildenhall in May 1981 featuring the wraparound camouflage scheme. It was originally delivered to the RAF on 5 May 1964 and also served with 101 and 44 Squadrons. It was scrapped at Waddington at the end of 1982. (*Philip Birtles photo*)

Waddington Wing Vulcan B.2 XM652 ready for its crew in September 1974. This aircraft was delivered to the RAF on 14 August 1964 and also served with the Coningsby and Cottesmore Wings, finally serving with 50 Squadron in the tanker role. (*Philip Birtles photo*)

The final production Vulcan B.2 XM657 operating with 44 Squadron at RAF Waddington in May 1981. It is seen landing with the wing mounted airbrakes extended and also features the wraparound camouflage. This aircraft was delivered on 14 January 1965, initially to 35 Squadron and operated from Cottesmore and Waddington. It was finally flown from Waddington to Manston on 5 January 1982 for fire fighting training. (*Philip Birtles photo*)

Although the Vulcan fleet was on Central Servicing which meant that individual squadron identities were not carried, for the Queen's Silver Jubilee at Finningley on 29 July 1977, aircraft from every RAF unit were represented with their unit badge. Examples of the Vulcan fleet included SR.2 XH534 of 27 Squadron, B.2 XH559 of 230 OCU marked up as 35 Squadron, XM651 of 50 Squadron and B.2 XM605 of 101 Squadron Waddington Wing. The latter aircraft was flown to Castle Air Force Base in California on 8 September 1981 for display in the USAF Museum. (*Philip Birtles photos*)

Vulcan B.2 XM648 of 44 Squadron
at Mildenhall in May 1981 painted
in the wraparound camouflage
scheme. XM648 served with the
Conningsby and Cottesmore Wings,
moving to Waddington Wing in
March 1968 where it was operated
by 101, IX and 44 Squadrons.
It was scrapped at Waddington
in December 1982.
(*Philip Birtles photo*)

Vulcan B.2 XM649 on readiness at
Waddington in September 1974.
It was one of four allocated to the
'Giant Voice' competition in the
USA, which is why a Union Jack
is displayed on the fin. XM649 was
delivered to the RAF on 13 May
1964 serving initially on the
Conningsby and Cottesmore Wings.
(*Philip Birtles photo*)

Vulcan B.2 XM649 at low level over Bomber Country, Lincolnshire. This aircraft operated latterly with the Waddington Wing and was flown to St Athan on 2 December 1982 for scrapping.
(BAE Woodford)

RIGHT: Vulcan B.2 about to touchdown with airbrakes deployed on 17 December 1982 at the close of service of this fine aircraft. This aircraft features dark grey undersides. (*RAF photo*)

LEFT: Vulcan B.2s XM607 in 44 Squadron markings, which flew Black Buck 1, leading a farewell formation over the lowlands of Lincolnshire – XM612 is nearest, XL391 of 44 Squadron on the starboard side and XM597 at the rear on 17 December 1982. XM607 is preserved at Waddington; XM612 has been preserved by the City of Norwich Aviation Museum; XL391 was delivered to Squires Gate Airport at Blackpool on 16 February 1983 but was scrapped in 2006 and XM597 was the aircraft which had to divert to Rio de Janeiro on Black Buck Six. XM597 was preserved with the Scottish Museum of Flight at East Fortune in 1983. (*RAF photo*)

LEFT: A detachment of four Vulcan B.2s of IX Squadron on deployment to warmer climates under inspection before making a stream departure from the ORP. (*MOD photo*)

LEFT: Vulcan B.2s XM598 of 50 Squadron and XM575 of 101 Squadron based at RAF Waddington form at high altitude during a training exercise in November 1976. Both of these aircraft have been preserved: XM598 to the Aerospace Museum at Cosford on 20 January 1983 and XM575 to the Leicester Air Museum at East Midlands Airport on 25 January 1983. (*MOD photo*)

LEFT: A pair of Vulcan B.2s, including XM571, at readiness at Waddington showing the contrast between the wraparound camouflage on the nearest aircraft and the light grey undersides on XM571.
(*Ian Allan Publishing collection*)

RIGHT: A Vulcan B.2 of the NEAF on approach to Akrotiri in Cyprus with a brace of Harriers of 1 Squadron deployed from Wittering at the ready. (*Rolls-Royce photo*)

Vulcan B.2 XH562 of 44 Squadron in the landing configuration with the wing mounted air brakes extended to reduce drag before the braking parachute was deployed after touch-down.
(*RAF Museum photo*)

Vulcan B.2 XM612 of 101 Squadron demonstrating the high power of the Olympus engines with a spirited take-off during a deployment to a hotter environment.
(*RAF Museum photo*)

RIGHT: Three Vulcan B.1s, XH476, XH475 and XA909 of 101 Squadron based at Waddington formate at high altitude, the environment they used for operation, until low level profiles were introduced.
(*BAE Woodford*)

ABOVE: 50 Squadron Vulcan BK.2 XH560 refuelling an RAF Tornado GR.1. (*RAF Museum photo*)

RIGHT: Following the Falklands War, a number of Vulcans were converted for flight refuelling duties. Vulcan BK.2 XL428 is refuelling BK.2 XH560, over the North Sea. (*BAE Heritage Centre photo*)

RIGHT: An ex-101 Squadron Vulcan BK.2 used for the development programme for the flight refuelling role. The underside of the aircraft has been painted white to make the red and black guide markings more prominent for the receiving aircraft. (*BAE Heritage Centre photo*)

ABOVE: A rear view of a Blue Steel stand-off missile hung under the belly of the Vulcan with the bomb bay doors recessed. To provide adequate ground clearance, the lower fin on the Blue Steel was folded up until ready for launch. (BAE Woodford)

LEFT: Newly camouflaged Vulcan B.2 XM645 in formation with the anti-flash white finish on XJ824 during the transition to low level duties. (BAE Woodford)

BELOW: During Blue Steel trials a number of instrumented aerodynamic full-scale models were tested, the release and flight profile being recorded by TV cameras. (BAE Woodford)

ABOVE: Vulcan B.1 XA903 was used for Blue Steel stand-off missile trials, with the weapon located in recessed doors under the bomb bay. (BAE Woodford)

RIGHT: Initially a pair of Skybolt missiles were to be mounted under the Vulcan wings, one each side, with a later option of two per side. The missile was fitted with a streamlined tail fairing to reduce drag, which was jettisoned before firing. Fitted on this occasion is an aerodynamic test round. (BAE Woodford)

LEFT: The Blue Steel stand off missile system had a range of ground equipment for handling the weapon, including a special trolley for mounting it under the aircraft. (BAE Woodford)

ABOVE: Vulcan B.1 XA903 making a high altitude test firing of the Avro Blue Steel stand-off guided missile. *(BAE Woodford)*

RIGHT: Rear view of the Blue Steel installation beneath Vulcan Mk.1 XA903. *(BAE Woodford)*

ABOVE: Vulcan B.2 XJ783 in the overall anti-flash white finish for high altitude combat operations. *(BAE Woodford)*

LEFT: Camouflaged Vulcan B.2 XL446 carrying a Blue Steel stand-off missile with the Scampton Wing, which was responsible for maintaining the nuclear deterrent until it was taken over by the Royal Navy with the Trident nuclear armed submarines. *(BAE Woodford)*

ABOVE: The second production Vulcan B.Mk.2 XH534 at high level in the original overall white finish. (BAE Woodford)

RIGHT: The second production Vulcan B.Mk.2 XH534 in low level camouflage finish. (BAE Woodford)

RIGHT: Vulcan B.2 XH558 was one of the aircraft converted to the BK.2 flight refuelling configuration for service with 50 Squadron. (BAE Woodford)

BELOW: A comparison of Britain and the USA's answer to the strategic bomber requirement. Vulcan B.2 XH535 flies in formation with a USAF B-52 during an exercise in the USA. While the Vulcan has been out of service with the RAF for some 25 years, the B-52 still soldiers on. (BAE Woodford)

LEFT: Vulcan B.2 XM575 of 44 Squadron at low level. (*BAE Woodford*)

RIGHT AND OVERLEAF: Vulcan B.2 XM575 of 44 Squadron over its home base of Waddington a few miles south of Lincoln, where further Vulcans are parked on the airfield. Waddington was a major World War 2 bomber base with Lancasters and was the final operational base for the Vulcans. It is now home to the Sentry AEW.1s of 8/23 Squadrons, Nimrod R.1s of 51 Squadron and the new Sentinel R.1s of 5 Squadron, all on intelligence gathering duties. (*BAE Heritage Centre photo*)

4

Black Buck
Vulcan Attack on the Falklands

The Vulcan covered twenty miles in three minutes as the navigators lined up with the target, the last ten miles being a stable flight to ensure accuracy with the bomb doors open. The short-range radar from the defending Skyguard had detected the incoming bomber and the Vulcan's crew spoofed the anti-aircraft guns with ECM. The first bomb was released two miles from the target, the last leaving five seconds later.

Argentina's aggressive intentions were first signalled by the landing of scrap merchants and infantry on South Georgia in March 1982, followed by the invasion of the Falklands on 2 April. The British Government, led by Prime Minister Margaret Thatcher, immediately reacted to this hostile act against the British Overseas Territory by ordering a taskforce known as Operation Corporate to be formed by the Royal Navy and the army and an air strike force led by the RAF.

The only aircraft with the capacity and potential range to reach the Falklands was the Vulcan, supported by a flight of refuelling Victor tankers. However, it was not a simple solution. The Vulcans had relinquished their conventional bombing role some ten years previously and were configured as tactical nuclear bombers. The Vulcan force had not practiced flight refuelling for twenty years and there were no personnel in service that had the necessary experience. The Vulcan force, based at Waddington, consisted of four units: IX, 44, 50 and 101 Squadrons. The remaining Vulcans were due to be withdrawn on 1 July, with some redundant aircraft being scrapped on the far side of the airfield, while others had retired to museums. Although no definite target had been selected, the Vulcan squadrons were called to standby.

On 2 April, Waddington had instructions to prepare ten Vulcans for the conventional free-fall bombing role and flight-refuelling systems were refitted: the refuelling probes had been covered with araldite but twenty new non-return valves were fortunately located in store at RAF Stafford. The four squadrons consisted of eight Vulcans each, all possessing unique flying and operational characteristics due to their hand-built nature, age and lack of investment in the updating of the fleet. The Navigation and Bomb Systems (NBS) were antiquated analogue systems with no assistance from inertial navigation (INS). It was therefore necessary to select the aircraft that flew well and would drop bombs accurately.

The Vulcans would carry over ten tons of high explosive iron bombs with full fuel, taking the aircraft close to, or over, its normal all-up flying weight. As a consequence, the Vulcans would require the 20,000lb thrust Olympus 301 engines which were not fitted to all of the aircraft in the fleet. The selected crews were required to train on flight refuelling operations and qualify by day and night on receiving fuel, while the Victor force which had been called to standby at Marham, would also have to train in the receiving of fuel by day and night, since at the time their task was only to dispense fuel. Such demands limited the

A pair of 50 Squadron Vulcan BK.2s, XH560 and XL426, practice air-to-air refuelling over the North Sea.
(BAE Woodford)

number of Victors available for Vulcan flight refuelling training to three crews only, plus one in reserve.

With Ascension Island in the mid-Atlantic as the only staging post, the distances of 4000 miles were way beyond the normal operating range of the Vulcan or Victor. Not only would they face the need to refuel, but to succeed, an attack would have to be conducted at low-level to avoid the Argentine defences that were an unknown quantity at the time, and it was also believed that the Vulcan's electronic counter measures (ECM) would be ineffective as it was geared to repel Soviet systems in Eastern Europe.

Three crews were selected for the bombing run, led by Flight Lieutenant Martin Withers, Squadron Leader John Reeve and Squadron Leader Monty Montgomery with Neil McDougall in reserve, the latter not benefiting from full training. The aircraft allocated were XM597, XM598 and XM607. The Vulcan flight decks were very basic with no luxuries such as galleys or toilets. Like the Vulcans, the supporting Victor tankers were nearing the end of their service lives, with four to five aircraft only being available on any one day. Such restrictions would have to change drastically in support of the Falklands operation. With no current use for 1000lb iron bombs, stocks had been gradually run down and 167 were found for both training and combat purposes.

A number of bombs had been manufactured with cast iron cases which would shatter on impact and be of no use in damaging a runway. The tougher machined cases were therefore necessary for the mission. These bombs would burrow into the ground and create an earthquake effect on explosion, making it impossible to repair a runway in the short term.

To convert the Vulcans to the conventional bombing role required the sourcing and installation of suitable bomb holders and release sequence mechanisms, some of which were acquired from a scrap contractor: one essential part for the bomb-aiming equipment was used as an ashtray in the engineers' mess at Waddington; a seal for a new radar-jamming device was improvised from corks from a home-brew beer kit. A number of ex-BA VC-10s were stored at Abingdon allowing the removal of the twin Carousel INS which would assist the crews in locating the Falklands after flying more than 4000 miles over featureless ocean; astro navigation could not be relied upon with sufficient accuracy. Therefore, to provide an effective defence in a high-risk environment, ECM pods were borrowed from the Buccaneer fleet at Honington.

The first four Victors were deployed to Ascension Island on 18 April, with five aircraft arriving the day after. The remote island made it possible for a specially configured Victor supported by

FAR LEFT: The ECM pod fitted under the Vulcan starboard wing which was borrowed from the Buccaneer fleet at Honington, and was successful in spoofing Argentine radars in the Falklands. (*AHB/MOD photo*)

LEFT: Vulcan B.2 being prepared for another sortie to the Falklands with the loading of 1000lb bombs on Ascension Island. (*AHB/MOD photo*)

ABOVE: One of the Black Buck Vulcans taking on fuel from a Victor tanker during Operation Corporate. (*AHB/MOD photo*)

ABOVE RIGHT: A pair of Victor BK.2s flight refuelling in support of Black Buck operations on the Falkland Islands. (*AHB/MOD photo*)

four others in the tanker role to make a reconnaissance flight over South Georgia. This mission confirmed that there were no enemy surface ships in the area and also helped prove the concept of tanker support in the South Atlantic. While the original plan had been to attack the Falklands from 300 feet at 350 knots, the threat of Oerlikon radar-directed 35mm cannons and Roland air defence missiles made this approach particularly hazardous. Although it was not confirmed until the last minute, it was assumed that the Stanley runway would be the target. Therefore it was decided to modify the attack profile of the Vulcans to a low 300 feet approach over the sea just before dawn. They would then climb to 8000 feet over the target, later increased to 10,000 feet, and release the bombs in a stick 35 degrees to the runway heading to ensure at least some would hit the target.

On 29 April, the Vulcans left Waddington for Ascension Island loaded with twenty-one 1000lb bombs of World War 2 design. The noise of the departure interrupted the disbandment ceremony of IX Squadron, which was to be reformed as a Tornado unit. The Vulcans, flown by Reeve and Withers, were supported by five Victors operated by relatively inexperienced crews since the main force was already stationed at Wideawake Airfield in Ascension Island. By this time there were fourteen Victor tankers of 55 and 57 Squadrons at Ascension Island, more than half the total RAF fleet.

The plan was for two Vulcans and eleven Victors to take-off together with four Victors forming two flights each in a carefully designed pyramid of support. The three remaining Victors would accompany one of the Vulcans in the third flight, while one Vulcan would be held in reserve. John Reeve and his crew in XM598 were the prime Vulcan attack team with Martin Withers in XM607 as reserve. The reserve Vulcan, flown by Withers, would return after a successful refuelling at the first bracket together with four Victors which had completed the transfer of fuel.

At the second bracket, two Victors would top up the other two Victors and the Vulcan before returning to Ascension Island. This was followed by a Victor to Victor transfer followed by a final Victor to Vulcan transfer with less than 1000 miles to the target. On the return after the bomb run, a Victor tanker would meet the Vulcan at a rendezvous east of Rio de Janeiro to

LEFT: Vulcan B.2 XM597 of 50 Squadron at dispersal. This aircraft served with 12 Squadron at Coningsby, followed by 9 Squadron at Cottesmore. It then served with the Waddington Wing and participated in the Black Buck operations, during which it had to divert to Rio de Janeiro due to the probe breaking while linking up for a fuel transfer. This Vulcan is now preserved at The Museum of Flight at East Fortune in Scotland. (*BAE Heritage Centre photo*)

RIGHT: A pair of Vulcan B.2s at unusually high altitude. (*BAE Heritage Centre photo*)

ABOVE: Victor BK.2 XL161 of 55 Squadron at Boscombe Down in June 1992, of the type which refuelled the Vulcans on the strikes in Operation Corporate ten years before. (*Philip Birtles photo*)

LEFT: A Victor BK.2 of 57 Squadron returns to Widewake Airfield on the volcanic Ascension Island using the brake parachute to avoid loading on the brakes, after providing support to Operation Corporate. (*AHB/MOD photo*)

provide fuel for the return flight to Ascension Island. The logistics of how fuel was transferred from tankers to bombers was worked out by the crews the night before using four slide-rules and a calculator.

From the very outset, the mission came close to failure. At 23.00hrs on 30 April 1982, the attack fleet left Ascension Island, but soon after take-off, XM598 had to abort due to a pressure seal failure in a DV window, making XM607, originally the reserve aircraft, the sole bomber. As the aircraft flew south, the crew realised that the fuel calculations were inaccurate and that the Vulcan would be short of fuel, therefore a number of outbound tankers were forced to turn round on their return to

Ascension Island. The transfer of fuel from the final pair of Victors coincided with a high-altitude violent thunderstorm. After being refuelled from the first Victor, the second plane broke its probe on the basket of its partner, resulting in it being unable to take on any further fuel. Fortunately, there was sufficient fuel to make a safe return to Ascension Island. The two Victors changed position, the damaged plane departing for base.

This left the two remaining aircraft low on fuel, with the Vulcan 7000lb short. In radio silence, the Victor turned for base in the hope of finding a tanker before running out of fuel, with no explanation being given to a puzzled Martin Withers. Withers put the Vulcan into a dive, levelling out at 300 feet over the sea. The Vulcan lacked an up-to-date pressure setting and the radio altimeters were accurate only to within 250 feet, which left a highly hazardous margin above the sea. Meanwhile, the two INS systems were showing diverging signals, the decision being made to take the mean, hoping to bring the Falklands into view.

When the crew believed that they were getting close to the target, Withers pulled up slightly, momentarily exposing the aircraft to enemy radar. As the Vulcan climbed, the HS2 identified high ground ahead, confirming that after eight hours in the air, they were within one mile off track. Forty miles from the target, the Vulcan climbed to 10,000 feet in full view of the Argentine radar as it made its final approach. Thankfully for the Vulcan's crew, the defenders were not alert and did not take the bomber's radar signal seriously and little was done to identify it – surprise was complete.

The Vulcan covered twenty miles in three minutes as the navigators lined up with the target, the last ten miles being a stable flight to ensure accuracy with the bomb doors open. The short-range radar from the defending Skyguard had detected the incoming bomber and the Vulcan's crew spoofed the anti-aircraft guns with ECM. The first bomb was released two miles from the target, the last leaving five seconds later. Withers pulled away in a climbing turn to port before the first bomb hit the target 18 seconds after release and the Vulcan was by then out of range of the defending guns. The target had been hit. The runway and surrounding areas of the airfield were severely damaged, making it impossible for fast jet operations. The mission had also made it absolutely clear to the Argentine forces that the RAF could attack them.

Damage to the runway and installations at Port Stanley following the bombs dropped by Vulcan XM607 on the Black Buck One raid. (*AHB/MOD photo*)

RIGHT: Squadron Leader Reeve and his crew operated Black Buck Two in XM607 dropping twenty-one 1000lb bombs on Stanley Airfield, damaging installations, but not hitting the runway. There is evidence of temporary repairs to the runway after the first raid. (*RAF Museum photo*)

ABOVE: For the Black Buck operations against the Argentine forces in the Falklands, amongst the Vulcan weapons loads were twenty-one 1000lb iron bombs used for cratering the runway at Port Stanley. (*BAE Woodford*)

FAR RIGHT: Vulcan B.2 XM607 from the Waddington Wing returning to Wideawake Airfield on the volcanic island of Ascension following the successful completion of Black Buck One by Flight Lieutenant Martin Withers and his crew. (*RAF Museum photo*)

Meanwhile, the final Victor was heading back to Ascension Island with insufficient fuel to reach its destination, and the Vulcan was on course for the Rio RV in the hope of a refuelling rendezvous. The Victor was four hours from base when a signal was received that a tanker was on its way to meet them. However, the Vulcan was in a far tighter spot with less than one hour of fuel remaining. The returning Victor made a successful linkage with the tanker and returned safely to Wideawake Airfield. The thirsty Vulcan – much to the relief of its crew – made the rendezvous with the Victor that trailed its hose forty miles ahead of the bomber, transferring 36,000lb of its 70,000lb of fuel. The connection was made after the third attempt 200 miles south of the planned RV, and although there was a fuel leak that caused visibility difficulties, Withers decided to stay with the contact in case a further one failed.

Bob Tuxford, who flew the final Victor, landed at Wideawake after 14 hours in the air. Vulcan XM607 returned to Ascension Island after 15 hours and 45 minutes over the South Atlantic, the longest bombing mission ever conducted by the RAF. Experiences from this first bombing run showed that excessive fuel consumption was caused by the varying altitudes and manoeuvring in formation with the Victor tanker aircraft, and mindful of this, further Black Buck missions were flown.

XM607 took part in Black Buck Two on 3-4 May, this time with a different crew, led by Squadron Leader Reeve. The Vulcan carried another load of twenty-one 1000lb bombs that resulted in damage to installations on the Stanley airfield but missed hitting the runway. Black Buck Three was cancelled due to strong headwinds *en route*. Black Buck Four was flown on 28-29 May in XM597 by a crew led by Squadron Leader McDougall, its payload consisting of four underwing AGM-45A Shrike anti-radar missiles. The intended target was the Argentine radar systems located around Port Stanley, but the mission was aborted when one of the Victors suffered a mechanical failure before the fuel transfer, and all aircraft returned to Ascension Island. Black Buck Five was scheduled with the same aircraft and crew on 30-31 May. The mission was in coordination with Harrier jet fighters while the AEO attempted to identify targets and three Shrikes were fired with indeterminate results.

Another attempt to destroy Argentine radar was made as Black Buck Six on 2-3 June with the same crew, but without the support of the Harriers as there were no hostiles to track. Two Shrikes were launched and reports suggest one may have damaged a radar antenna with a near miss. On the return to Ascension Island, the Vulcan connected with its Victor tanker at the RV, but as the probe was inserted into the drogue, there was a loud noise and the probe fractured at its weak point. With insufficient fuel to reach Ascension Island, and with no way of obtaining more, the planned alternative was a diversion to Rio de Janeiro in Brazil.

The crew began to dispose of classified material and attempts were made to jettison the two remaining Shrikes, but one missile refused to leave its mounting, and an emergency landing was made with only five minutes' worth of fuel left in the tanks. The Brazilian authorities removed the remaining Shrike and the Vulcan and its crew were held for a week before being allowed to return to Waddington, on the condition that the aircraft and crew were not used for further operations against the Falklands. Black Buck Seven was flown by Flight Lieutenant Withers on 12 June in XM607 with a combined payload of 1000lb HE and anti-personnel bombs. The targets were Argentine troop concentrations around Port Stanley and was claimed to be a partial success; all aircraft returned home to Ascension Island safely.

44 Squadron stayed in operation at Waddington until December 1982 to ensure that Argentina would not attempt further acts of aggression against the Falklands after their final surrender on 19 June.

RIGHT: Vulcan B.2 XM606 of the Waddington Wing which flew the Black Buck One operation in the Falklands, dropping twenty-one 1000lb bombs on the airfield at Port Stanley. (*BAE Woodford*)

RIGHT: Vulcan B.2 XM597 at Ascension on return from Black Buck Four with Nimrods in the background. (*AHB/MOD photo*)

LEFT: Vulcan B.2 with an AGM-45A Shrike anti-radar missile mounted under the wing on the Skybolt pick-up points, as used against Argentine radars in the Falklands. (*RAF Museum photo*)

Often referred to as the 'Little People's Aircraft' due to the high level of support it receives from the public, Vulcan B.2 XH558 at Bruntingthorpe is probably the largest and most complex project in the world to return an aircraft to flight status.

Often referred to as the 'Little People's Aircraft' due to the high level of support it receives from the public, Vulcan B.2 XH558 at Bruntingthorpe is probably the largest and most complex project in the world to return an aircraft to flight status. With the retirement of the last operational Vulcan from service on 31 March 1984, the RAF formed the Vulcan Display Flight (VDF) which was based at Waddington initially, operating XL426. When the aircraft reached the stage where a major overhaul was required, it was retired to Southend on 19 December 1986 where the Vulcan Restoration Trust kept it in working condition.

Vulcan B.Mk.2 XH558 had made its maiden flight from Woodford on 21 May 1960. As the first of the upgraded version to enter service with the RAF, it was delivered to 230 Operational Conversation Unit (OCU) on 1 July 1960 at Waddington. The aircraft joined the Waddington Wing, consisting of 44, 50 and 101 Squadrons in February 1968. It was converted into a B.2(MRR) maritime reconnaissance configuration in August 1973 for service with 27 Squadron at Scampton in September 1974. With the demand for additional flight refuelling tankers during the Falklands conflict, and while VC-10s were being converted to the role, six Vulcans were converted to tankers, including XH558. The aircraft returned to Woodford on 29 June 1982 for conversion to the K.2 configuration and was allocated to 50 Squadron at Waddington on 12 October 1982.

It was withdrawn from use on 17 September 1984, but selected for display duties with the VDF at Waddington and returned to its B.2 configuration ready for its debut at Bournemouth in May 1985. It thrilled the airshow crowds as a star performer for some seven years until its farewell display at Cranfield on 20 September 1992. It was then put up for disposal and acquired by the Walton family with delivery to Bruntingthorpe on 23 March 1993 in what was believed to be its last flight. Led by David Walton, the aircraft was maintained in taxiing condition, making power runs along the long Bruntingthorpe runway, together with other combat jets including English Electric Lightnings on special open days.

When the Vulcan was sold, the package consisted of 17.5 tons of spares including eight engines and over 170,000 items that were managed and recorded by the fifteen to twenty strong group of volunteers. These dedicated enthusiasts who perform non-Vulcan duties are essential to the restoration project as they assist the skilled engineers in undertake more productive tasks. In 1997, a team lead by Dr Robert Pleming began to create a feasibility plan to return XH558 to the air, phase one being a technical survey by The Vulcan Operating Company (TVOC). Pleming had vital support from the Heritage Committee of BAE Systems who provided the information for type design approval, essential for Civil Aviation Authority (CAA) approval.

In 1998, the Walton family had to make the difficult decision to convert XH588 from a ground-running attraction to a fully operational aircraft, as the Vulcan would have to be dismantled before restoration to flying condition, leaving it to remain derelict if funding was not achieved. The last taxi run was made in public at Bruntingthorpe on 5 September 1999.

Vulcan to the Sky (VTS) commenced fundraising in 2001, with an application to the Heritage Lottery Fund (HLF) following

Vulcan to the sky! Thanks to the hard work and dedication of the VTS, it is hoped that XH558 will return to the skies in summer 2007. (*Philip Birtles photo*)

a year later. This was rejected in November 2002 because it concentrated more on the safety aspects and did not include sufficient educational proposals. It is well known that the HLF do not support the operation of flying aircraft, but this does not stop them approving the engineering scheme to return the aircraft to flight status providing there is a good educational programme. In this case, the educational programme is based on The Cold War which is now part of the schools' curriculum. There was a public outcry when the VTS proposal was turned down, but with the help of the HLF, a second successful bid was lodged in 2003, with £2,734,000 being awarded on 23 June 2004.

In addition, a further £1 million had been raised by supporters, allowing work to start in 2005. To bring confidence to the project, XH558 was purchased for the nation by VTS from the Walton family who continue to be enthusiastic supporters, including supplying the hangar for a modest rent. A funding crisis announced on 1 August 2006, warned that if sufficient funds were not raised with some urgency, work would have to stop and the restoration team made redundant by 31 August; a further £1.2 million was required to complete the restoration to flight status.

Plans were put in hand to have a publicity roll-out from the hangar on 31 August on what may have been the final exhibition for XH558. Meanwhile, further efforts were made to raise the extra funds with £500,000 pledged or donated from the public. When the Vulcan's plight was announced on BBC Breakfast TV, followed by a last minute donation by Sir Jack Hayward of a further £500,000, 31 August had become a celebration rather than a wake.

Both BAE Systems and Rolls-Royce provide technical support from Chadderton and Filton respectively; Dave Nadin from BAE attends to the restoration two days a week to assist with design information and support. Rolls-Royce are unable to provide overhaul facilities for the Olympus engines as they no longer exist, therefore the flying programme is entirely dependent on the 'nil life' Olympus engines that were acquired in the original deal. Other engines are of an unknown quantity and suitable for ground-running only.

In 1999, the feasibility study commenced and original equipment suppliers were approached. Many pledged their support to the project, but in the intervening period some companies had become unable to help as their circumstances had changed. Examples of some of the many companies who have supported the return of XH558 to the sky, in addition to BAE and R-R were Goodrich with tyres, brakes, alternators and the auxiliary power unit (APU); powered flying controls by Boulton Paul; Kersley who rebuilt the undercarriage units on behalf of Dowty/Messier, who remain the design authority; Beagle Aviation who refurbished the flying controls; Dunlop who were responsible for hoses and valves; Kidde-Graviner for the fire systems; Serco who overhauled the instrument panels, avionics and safety equipment; parachutes by Irvin. The manufacturers were able to support the project by providing £1.2 million of work in kind and 160 to 170 companies supplied free goods and services. It is believed that the flying control restoration has been the most demanding of the many activities undertaken.

BELOW AND OPPOSITE: Vulcan B.Mk.2 XH558 of the Vulcan Display Flight (VDF) at Mildenhall in May 1990 and Boscombe Down in June 1992. A sight hoped to be seen again in 2007 when it should be back in the air on the display circuit. (*Philip Birtles photo*)

ABOVE AND OPPOSITE: Vulcan B.2
XH558 of the VDF giving spirited
displays at Mildenhall and
Boscombe Down – a sight which
hopefully will be repeated from 2007
providing sufficient corporate
sponsorship can be found.
(*Philip Birtles photo*)

With BAE not wishing to be involved directly, Marshall Aerospace, as an M5 approved organisation, were appointed to take overall manufacturing responsibility. The TVOC, conceived by David Walton as the engineering division of C Walton Ltd (who own Bruntingthorpe airfield), provide the manpower for the project, while Marshall Aerospace hold the Permit for Maintenance Release (PMR) giving the necessary approvals to achieve the requirements of the Civil Airworthiness Authority (CAA). TVOC employs twelve engineering staff who are supported by twelve airframe contractors and two electrical contractors as well as a dozen engineers from Marshall Aerospace. Although the use of Marshall is a costly part of the exercise, the company has unique expertise, including design authority in the challenging area of converting military aircraft to civil status. The overall programme is supported by a dozen administration staff covering marketing/PR, fundraising, commercial activities and HR functions.

The main structural challenge was to extend the fatigue life of the airframe, the Vulcan being a simple structure based on the technology of the Avro Shackleton and Lancaster heavy bomber. The main challenge was Modification 2222, which was the strengthening of the rear lower wing spar attachment. With this modification, the Vulcan is now classified as in new condition as far as the fatigue index is concerned. Work on the future winter overhauls will continue to maintain the fatigue index, measurements being taken from two fatigue counters in the bomb bay. Also, a weapons specialist was being sought to cover the maintenance of the ejector seats.

Apart from the removal of nine miles of redundant wiring, including 47 systems, other major work has included the rewiring of the remaining systems and corrosion control. Although the aircraft is in excellent condition having been kept under cover for much of its life, corrosion was found in the wing skins over the main undercarriage bays, resulting in the replacement of stringers. The CAA have been very supportive with the restoration of the Vulcan, having a high level of confidence in the abilities and professionalism of the team responsible. Also, all active members are experienced with the RAF methodology and are familiar with the use of Air Publications, which helped build a solid confidence with the CAA.

BELOW LEFT, BELOW AND OPPOSITE: Vulcan B.2 XH558 of VDF landing and taxiing to its parking spot following a demonstration at Boscombe Down in June 1992 at the International Air Tattoo. (*Philip Birtles photo*)

The aircraft is classed in the 'complex category' as there is no manual backup for the systems, including power controls and electrics; with the defence systems removed, including the navigation equipment and H2S radar, the maximum all-up weight (auw) is reduced to 146,000lb. The TVOC engineers helped Marshall devise a suitable training programme, which they had to pass in all three subjects: airframes, propulsion and electrics/avionics and ongoing maintenance. Flight limitations are to be a maximum ceiling of 17,500 ft and a normal cruise of 250 knots, increasing to 300 in an emergency. All manoeuvres will be limited to 1g to avoid any overstressing, flying on energy rather than power to reduce cycles on the engines – a cycle is from nil power to full power and return to zero.

With the return to flight status, the next challenge is to provide a qualified crew capable of operating the aircraft. With the last flight being undertaken fourteen years ago, there is a serious lack of pilots who are suitable to fly XH558, nor is there a simulator to assist in gaining experience (note: a PC flight simulator is available, RAF Vulcan, which is fully licensed by the RAF and a proportion of the sale price is donated to the Vulcan

to the Sky project). With all redundant defensive and offensive systems removed there is no requirement for the navigators, leaving two pilots and an AEO as crew. For flights where the Vulcan is to land at other airfields, a crew chief will also be carried. The chief pilot is Dave Thomas, who was the last pilot to fly the Vulcan into Bruntingthorpe. Presently, there are four pilots and three AEOs available with more aircrew being brought up to date to cover the flying life of the aircraft. The current lead AEO is Barry Masefield with Kevin 'Taff' Stone as crew chief throughout 2007 and 2008, followed by Alan Rolfe for the 2009 season. All aircrew are not only Vulcan qualified but require the appropriate civilian licences.

Pre-flight training is being conducted with the generous help of the owners of 'live' Vulcans XM655 and XL426 at Wellesbourne Mountford and Southend, where systems operation and emergency procedures can be practised. The flight training will be combined with the CAA test phase and include Marshall and CAA test pilots who will be responsible for clearing the aircraft for civil operations. Ground crew training will result in eight, type-rated engineers and, as an additional benefit, six to eight RAF technicians will train in each practical trade for six weeks at a time. As previously mentioned, the planned flying life of ten years depends upon the life of the engines, estimated to be 2,000 hours each or 1,200 cycles.

At the time of writing in March 2007, the plan was a short flight between April and May. Its first public appearance was to fly down The Mall and over Buckingham Palace on 17 June to celebrate the 25th anniversary of the Falklands War. However, this was not possible due to delays in the completion of the restoration. The maiden flight is planned for summer 2007 but before it can be approved for public display it will have to complete 10 hours of flight.

The average airshow cannot afford to pay a commercial rate for the Vulcan since each flight costs £100,000 including test flights and training, and £1.2 million is required annually to operate the aircraft for around 40 hours. The restoration to fly is only part of an ongoing programme requiring further financing. Therefore a major sponsor, or group of sponsors, are necessary to finance the operation of this fine example of Britain's aerospace heritage, and more airshows and events will be attended from 2008 to publicise the sponsor's contribution.

LEFT: Vulcan Display Flight Vulcan B.2 XH558 noses in close to the camera ship. (BAE Woodford)

LEFT: Vulcan Display Flight Vulcan B.2 XH558 in a dramatic view during a display. When XH558 returns to the air, the manoeuvres will be limited to 1g and using available energy. *(BAE Woodford)*

ABOVE: Vulcan B.2 XH558 in the hanger at Bruntingthorpe in a dismantled state with the model of a Vulcan used in the James Bond movie *Thunderball*. *(VTS photo)*

LEFT: One of the eight unused Olympus engines being prepared for fitting into XH558 which hopefully will last for some 2,000 flying hours. (*VTS photo*)

BELOW: The jet pipe of number three Olympus engine being withdrawn for inspection and rectification from XH558. (*VTS photo*)

LEFT: Vulcan B.2 XH558 is a good fit in its hangar at Bruntingthorpe which is provided by the Walton family. There is also adequate room available for workshop facilities, although the hangar is not heated in the winter. The Vulcan airbrakes are raised on the wing and the control surfaces removed for restoration. (*VTS photo*)

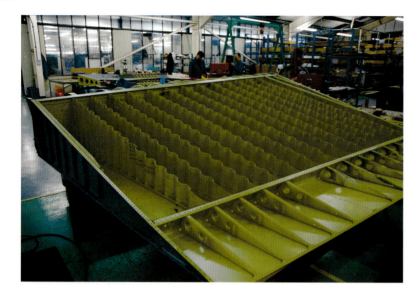

RIGHT: The rear lower wing spar attachment strengthened with Mod 2222 which extends the structural fatigue life of the aircraft, is bolted on to the spar flange. (*VTS photo*)

ABOVE AND LEFT: Before and after – the magnesium covered control surfaces suffered from corrosion and had to be completely restored and recovered by Beagle Aviation. (*VTS photo*)

RIGHT: The only way to repair wing skin corrosion was to peel the upper skin back to gain access. This was found to require the repair and replacement of stringers, and was only discovered at a fairly late stage in the return to flight programme. Engineer Neil Roberts is seen in late January 2007 working on the cure of the corrosion over the starboard undercarriage bay. Because of the hand-built nature of the Vulcan, each side could differ, often requiring other structures to be removed to gain access in an area that was not designed for repairs. (*VTS photo*)

ABOVE: The beak-like nose of XH558 without the radome fitted in March 2007. The H2S radar has been removed showing the front pressure bulkhead. Also shown is the flight refuelling probe with interior pipe work which has been decommissioned as it will not be used in practice.
(*Philip Birtles photo*)

ABOVE: The power controls were overhauled by Boulton Paul, the original manufacturers. These were particularly important as the Vulcan has no manual reversion, leading to it being certificated in the complex category. (*Philip Birtles photo*)

LEFT: Vulcan XH558 was rolled out on 31 August 2006 to celebrate the successful raising of funds to complete its return to flight. The team in front of the aircraft had faced redundancy earlier in the month due to lack of money to finance the completion. An intensive money raising campaign was successful in achieving sufficient funds at this late stage, making the event a celebration instead of a wake.
(*VTS photo*)

Appendix 1

Preserved Vulcans

From its first appearance at Farnborough as demonstrated by Roly Falk, the Vulcan captured the imagination of the enthusiast and the public in general wherever it appeared. As a result, when the Vulcan fleet wereas being retired from active service (and perhaps more than any other type) examples were acquired by museums in Britain and overseas.

A number of these aircraft have been kept in good working order with the engines run regularly, and are are taxied along runways for the public to enjoy. Such examples are XL426 at Southend Airport and XM655 at Wellesbourne Mountford, in addition to XH558 being returned to flying condition at Bruntingthorpe. Where space is restricted, nose sections have been preserved instead, allowing visitors to experience the character of the flight deck.

LEFT: Vulcan B.2 XL426 of VRT taxiing at Southend on 5 August 2006. (*Phil Whalley photo via VRT*)

Mk	Serial	Location	Status
B.Mk.2	XH558	Vulcan to the Sky, Bruntingthorpe	Restored to flying condition
B.Mk.2	XJ823	Carlisle, Cumbria	Static display
B.Mk.2A	XJ824	IWM Duxford	Static display in 101 Squadron markings
B.Mk.2	XL318	RAF Museum, Hendon	Static display
B.Mk.2	XL319	NE Aircraft Museum, Sunderland	Static display
B.Mk.2A	XL360	Midland Air Museum, Coventry Airport	Static display
B.Mk.2	XL361	Goose Bay, Canada	Static display
B.Mk.2	XL391	Blackpool Airport	Scrapped 2006 due to corrosion
B.Mk.2	XL426	Vulcan Restoration Trust, Southend Airport	Functional aircraft with systems operational, engines running and taxiing condition
B.Mk.2	XM569	South Wales Aircraft Museum, Cardiff	Scrapped on closure of museum and nose section to Gloucester Aviation, Staverton
B.Mk.2	XM573	Offut AFB, Nebraska, USA	Static display
B.2A	XM575	Aeropark, East Midlands Airport	Static display, but systems active
B.2	XM594	Newark Air Museum, Winthorpe	Static display
B.2	XM597	Museum of Flight, East Fortune	Static display
B.2	XM598	RAF Museum, Cosford	Static display
B.2	XM603	603 Club, Woodford	Spares recovery for XH558
B.2	XM605	Castle AFB, California, USA	Static display
B.2	XM606	Barksdale AFB, Louisiana, USA	Static display
B.2	XM607	RAF Waddington	8779M, Black Buck 1 aircraft
B.2	XM612	City of Norwich Aviation Museum	Static display
B.2	XM655	Wellesbourne Mountford	Functional aircraft with systems operational, engines running and taxiing condition

Vulcan B.MK.2 XJ823 which last served with 27 Squadron was delivered to Carlisle on 21 January 1983 to Mr Tom Stoddart and is preserved at the Solway Aviation Museum. Although it looks good in this picture, close inspection regrettably reveals corrosion in the rear fuselage due to its constant exposure to the salty air from the nearby coastline. (*Philip Birtles photo*)

Vulcan B.Mk.2 XJ824 in the markings of 101 Squadron which was delivered from Waddington to the IWM at Duxford on 13 March 1982 by Fl Lt Martin Withers a few weeks before his attack on Port Stanley. This aircraft had spent much of its time exposed to the elements at Duxford, but is now under cover in the new AirSpace hangar. (*Philip Birtles photo*)

Vulcan B.2 XL360 was delivered from Waddington to Coventry Airport on 26 January 1982 for the Midlands Air Museum. It is seen parked on the airport apron in February 1983 awaiting its move on to the museum site. (*Philip Birtles photo*)

Vulcan B.2 XL391 in 44 Squadron markings was flown from Waddington to Blackpool Airport on 16 February 1983, the intention being to keep the aircraft in functional condition. It is photographed here in September 1987. However, lacking shelter from the salty environment, it deteriorated progressively and was broken up on site on 12 January 2006. (*Philip Birtles photo*)

Vulcan B.2 XL426/G-VJET is preserved by the Vulcan Restoration Trust (VRT) at Southend in fully functional condition apart from flying duties. It was capable of taxiing but this has been postponed to allow urgent maintenance. It was operated by the RAF Vulcan Display Flight (VDF) for the 1984 and 1985 seasons until replaced by XH558. It was delivered to Southend on 19 December 1986 when it was bought by Roy Jacobsen, who also bought XM655 which was delivered to Wellesbourne Mountford. Both aircraft suffered from neglect and were to be scrapped. However, XL426 was rescued by a group of local enthusiasts, securing its future, who gradually returned the Vulcan to working order. First engine runs were made in early 1994 and the aircraft moved under its own power for the first time on 7 October 1995. For events and news visit www.avrovulcan.com. (*Philip Birtles photo*)

Vulcan B.2 XM569 in the markings of 44 Squadron was delivered from Waddington to Cardiff Airport on 21 January 1983 for the Wales Aircraft Museum. Sadly, all their aircraft suffered from being exposed to the salty atmosphere and became neglected. The Vulcan and many other exhibits were scrapped when the museum closed in early 1996. (*Philip Birtles photo*)

Vulcan B.2 XM575 with 44 Squadron marks was flown from Waddington to East Midlands Airport on 25 January 1983 to join the Aeropark which is run entirely by volunteers. The Vulcan is kept in good working order with the systems operational.
(*Philip Birtles photo*)

Vulcan B.2 XM594 was flown from Waddington to the Newark Air Museum on 7 February 1983, landing on the disused runway in a modest snowstorm. The captain was Squadron Leader Neil McDougall, who undertook Black Buck Four, Five and Six, the latter ending as guests of the Brazilian Air Force in Rio. The Vulcan has spent the last twenty-four years in the open and the volunteers at Winthorpe are fighting a hard battle to keep the systems operating as well as fighting the ravages of corrosion. There are plans in hand to put the Vulcan, together with the Hastings and Shackleton, under cover, leaving room for some of the remaining smaller aircraft. It is displayed with a Blue Steel missile on a cradle under the wing.
(*Philip Birtles photo*)

LEFT: Vulcan B.2 XM603 of 44 Squadron was retired to its place of origin – Woodford on 12 March 1982, where it was later painted overall white. It was maintained in working condition until late 2006, and was then used as a spares source for XH558.
(BAE Woodford)

Vulcan B.2 XM598 with 44 Squadron markings was delivered from Waddington to Cosford on 20 January 1983 for display in the Aerospace Museum, replacing the earlier B.Mk.1 XA900 which had been scrapped due to corrosion. XM598 was to have been the prime Vulcan in Black Buck One, but was unserviceable due to lack of pressurisation after take-off. This Vulcan is now under cover in The Cold War Exhibition at Cosford, bringing together all three V-Bombers in one place.
(Philip Birtles photo)

Vulcan B.2 XM603 was delivered from Waddington to Woodford on 12 March 1982. It has been maintained in working order by a group of retired BAE engineers who painted the aircraft in its original overall white anti-flash finish. Due to exposure to the elements, which made the aircraft structurally unsafe, this aircraft is scheduled to be scrapped during 2007 but is being cannibalised for spares by TVOC at Bruntingthorpe.
(Philip Birtles photo)

LEFT: Camouflaged Vulcan B.2 XH558 which was operated by the Vulcan Display Flight (VDF) visited its place of origin at Woodford during one of the annual flying shows, when it was placed nose to nose with the resident Vulcan B.2 XM603 returned to the overall white finish. *(BAE Woodford)*

RIGHT: Dramatic night-time view of the white Vulcan B.2 XM603 and camouflaged XH558 of VDF at Woodford. *(Charles Toop photo)*

Vulcan B.2 XM607 has been preserved at RAF Waddington since it was grounded in 1983. Following the departure of XH558 to Bruntingthorpe, the engineers prepared XM607 for external display and is now located close to the perimeter alongside the A15 road with parking in the nearby viewing area. This is perhaps the most famous Vulcan, having operated Black Buck One in the Falklands War, and would surely make a fitting memorial to the many thousands of Bomber Command crews who paid the ultimate sacrifice during World War 2 (and who still have not been fully recognised). If this were ever to happen, the aircraft would need to be protected in a building so it will not corrode and be consigned to the scrapheap.
(Philip Birtles photo)

Vulcan B.2 XM612 was flown from Waddington to Norwich Airport on 30 January 1983 to join the City of Norwich Aviation Museum. This aircraft last served with 44 Squadron. (*Philip Birtles photo*)

Vulcan B.2 XM655/G-VULC was delivered from Waddington to Wellesbourne Mountford on 11 February 1984, one of the last RAF flights of the type, having served with 50 Squadron. It was parked unattended until brought under ownership of the airfield management and was restored to working order by Delta Engineering. It has also been repainted and moved again under its own power in 1996 although it is not planned to fly. This aircraft is used by the Vulcan aircrew at Bruntingthorpe for systems training in preparation for the flying of XH558. This picture was taken in August 1994 before work started on the restoration. (*Philip Birtles photo*)

Appendix 2   Vulcan Production

Number	Mark	Serials			
2	Prototypes	VX770, VX777			
25	B.Mk.1	XA889 – XA913			
20	B.Mk.1A	XH475 – XH483,	XH497 – XH506,	XH532	
89	B.Mk.2	XH533 – XH539,	XH554 – XH563,	XJ780 – XJ784,	XJ823 – XJ825,
		XL317 – XL321,	XL359 – XL361,	XL384 – XL392,	XL425 – XL427,
		XL443 – XL446,	XM569 – XM576,	XM594 – XM612,	XM645 – XM657

Appendix 3   Specification

	B.Mk.1	B.Mk.1A	B.Mk.2
Dimensions			
Wing span	99ft (30.15m)	99ft (30.15m)	111ft (33.83m)
Length (nose to tail)	92ft 9in	99ft 11in (30.45m)	99ft 11in (30.45m)
Height	26ft 1in (7.93m)	26ft 1in (7.93m)	27ft 2in (8.28m)
Wing area	3,554 sq ft (330.2 sq m)	3,554 sq ft (330.2 sq m)	3,964 sq ft (368.3 sq m)
Wheel track	31ft 3in	31ft 3in	31ft 3in
Weights			
Empty	125,000lb		
Maximum	167,000lb	167,000lb	250,000lb
Power plants			
	BS Olympus 101	BS Olympus 102/104	BS Olympus 201/301
Thrust			
	11,000lb/4,990 kg	12,000lb/5,443 kg	17,000lb/7,710 kg
		13,500lb/6,125 kg	20,000lb/9,072 kg
Performance			
Max speed	625 mph at 40,000ft	625 mph	645 mph at 36,000ft
Service ceiling	55,000ft	55,000ft	60,000ft
Range	3,450 miles	3,450 miles	4,600 miles
Armament	1 x 10,000lb Blue Danube or 21 x 1000lb iron bombs	1 x 10,000lb Blue Danube or 21 x 1000lb iron bombs	1 x Blue Steel standoff missile or 21 x 1000lb iron bombs

The nose wheel undercarriage, entry door and bomb-aimers visual sight on VTS Vulcan B.2 XL426 at Southend in April 2007 as the aircraft is prepared for its regular engine runs, which are essential to the continued conservation of the aircraft. (*Philip Birtles photo*)

LEFT: The VTS Vulcan B.2 XL426 at Southend features the passive radar warning receivers on top of the tail fin giving a squared-off appearance. The main ECM equipment was located in the enlarged rear fuselage fairing. (*Philip Birtles photo*)

The large bomb bay of VTS Vulcan B.2 XL426 with the doors open, facing forward. The aircraft was designed around this large compartment, which is reminiscent of the wartime Lancaster bomber produced from the same stable. (*Philip Birtles photo*)

RIGHT: As well as being fitted with flight refuelling probes above the nose radome, a number of Vulcans were equipped with a small thimble radome housing the terrain following radar (TFR) as seen on XL426 at Southend. (*Philip Birtles photo*)

BELOW: The distinctive Phase 2 wing leading edge shape on the starboard side of Vulcan B.2 XL426 at Southend. (*Philip Birtles photo*)

RIGHT: The flight deck of preserved Vulcan XM602 nose at Bruntingthorpe giving some indication of the limited vision available to the pilots. On either side of the four white throttle levers are the fighter-like control sticks, unique to a bomber aircraft. (*Philip Birtles photo*)

LEFT: The two navigators were located in the rear of the small pressurised compartment on the starboard side and centre facing aft. The only means of escape was by parachute through the main access door. In XH558, all the defensive capabilities have been removed and navigators will not be carried. (*Philip Birtles photo*)

RIGHT: The Air Electronics Officer (AEO) was located on the portside of the rear cabin facing aft and next to the navigators. He was usually first aboard to bring the systems to life ready to start the engines. In XH558, the AEO will also be a flight engineer, monitoring all systems. (*Philip Birtles photo*)

The Vulcan to the Sky Trust, a Registered Charity, has been set up:

- To preserve and protect Avro Vulcan XH558, and to return her to full flying order.
- To demonstrate and display the aircraft around the United Kingdom for the benefit of the public, and to conserve her as an asset in perpetuity as an important part of British heritage.
- To advance the education of the public, specifically engineers and aviators, of her origins and design, and the historical and social context of the Cold War years.
- To inspire the young in engineering and design.

If you wish to find out more about the Vulcan to the Sky Trust and its activities, please visit www.vulcantothesky.com